Schooled Bodies?
negotiating adolescent validation through press, peers and parents

Majella McSharry

Trentham Books

Stoke on Trent, UK and Sterling, USA

Trentham Books Limited

Westview House	22883 Quicksilver Drive
734 London Road	Sterling
Oakhill	VA 20166-2012
Stoke on Trent	USA
Staffordshire	
England ST4 5NP	

First published 2009

British Library Cataloguing-in-Publication Data
A catalogue record for this book is available from the British Library

ISBN: 978 1 85856 429 6

The author and Trentham Books would like to thank the Publication Assistance Fund at Dublin City University which contributed to the cost of publishing this book.

Designed and typeset by Trentham Print Design Ltd, Chester and printed in Great Britain by Page Bros (Norwich) Ltd.

Contents

CONTENTS

Acknowledgements

I would like to offer my sincere thanks to the following people for their support in writing this book. To my editor Dr. Gillian Klein for her unwavering guidance and encouragement. To Dr. Maeve O'Brien, St. Patrick's College Drumcondra for reviewing an early draft of this book. To Dr. Rebecca King-O'Riain, Dr. Anne Lodge and particularly Dr. G. Honor Fagan from NUI Maynooth for their expertise during this study and their enthusiasm for and help in turning it into a book. To all the staff in the School of Education Studies at Dublin City University, especially Dr. Brendan Walsh, for their interest and confidence in this work. To the National Children's Office for funding the research on which this book is based. Special thanks to my parents Matt and Maura, my sister Elizabeth and my fiancé Ger for everything they have done and continue to do for me. Finally a huge thank you to all of the delightful and insightful teenagers I spoke to and whose thoughts and stories inform this book.

Introduction

Is eating one bowl of brown rice a day the unavoidable reality of a child in the majority world or the dietary choice of a child in the western world? Is sporadic vomiting the involuntary plight of a cancer sufferer or the elected ritual of an insecure teenager? Is enduring physical labour to the point of pain an economic consequence for child slaves or a self-inflicted necessity for young exercise enthusiasts? How can the hand that the former in each case appear to have been so harshly dealt be almost identical to the hand that the latter seeks out and utilises? When a western teenager resorts to eating minute amounts or purges after eating, or works out to the point of sheer exhaustion, this may be viewed as not unusual. On the contrary, these practices are often seen as an inevitable aspect of adolescents' normal obsessions with physical perfection.

There seems to be a general lay consensus that adolescence is a life period where concerns relating to the body are at a particular high. According to Fingerson:

> The sociology of the body and the sociology of childhood have developed substantially in recent years, often along parallel lines. However, there is little contact between these two fields. (2005:91)

'Older children ('teenagers') and their bodies' are particularly neglected in the sociology of childhood (*ibid*). This book is based on a study which connects the sociology of the body with the sociology of adolescence. It explores adolescence as an embodied period and examines how popular press, peers and parents school adolescents on how to understand their bodies during this period.

Memories of childhood and adolescence

I grew up in a village in rural Ireland, where I attended the local co-educational primary school. From a very early age I could see that the boys and girls in my class were quite different in shape and size. Some were tall and others were small; some were slight while others carried weight.

I was quite an active child with a passion for dancing. This, accompanied by a genuine disinterest in consuming large amounts of food, meant that I was always fairly slim. From an early age, therefore, I was aware that I had a particular type of body and learned that I could use my bodily talents for self-expression. While the other children in my class did not comment on my shape or size, they did so about some of my peers. Throughout my primary schooling I learned that overweight boys and girls were singled out and teased. They were called names to their faces by boys and behind their backs by girls. As we reached an age where boys became less intolerable, their opinion began to matter more to the girls in my class. Some began to diet intensively or exercise vigorously to loose weight. Some took pride in being able to rhyme off the exact amount of calories various bars of chocolate and packets of crisps contained. Somehow they seemed more validated by these regulated practices, even at ten and eleven years old.

In the early 1990s I went on to attend a single-sex girls' secondary school. By this point, most of the girls in my class were frequently thinking, or talking about, their bodies and those of others. They huddled over magazines talking about the bodies they admired. Some became obsessive about dieting and would refer to other girls' seemingly effortless slenderness with great resentment. Many were often thinner than the girls they were referring to, but could not see reason on this. Some girls grew very frustrated trying to fathom why their body was so different, while others grew frustrated trying to explain to them that their body was quite unlike how they saw it. It was almost impossible not to become engulfed in some form of bodily comparisons, concerns or uncertainties.

It seemed that boys my age were not free from body worries either. One of the most popular boys I knew was fun loving, intelligent, musically talented and a gifted footballer. However, during his time in secondary school, he acquired braces to straighten his teeth. This totally transformed his bubbly, energetic personality and he became introverted and shy. He obviously found this new embodied experience complex and difficult. Later in my schooling I was friendly with a guy who appeared to be the most confident person I had ever met. However, I soon discovered that he saw himself as being much heavier than his other friends and regularly used self-induced vomiting after eating. His girlfriend at the time had just lost two stone (13 kilo) in weight through compulsive exercising. Another friend of mine was taking strong medication to overcome problems because of his acne. His girlfriend had just had her navel pierced and was coping with the accompanying tenderness and taking measures to avoid infection. Could I really be among a unique group of peers on a quest to have their bodies validated in some way? Working as a second level teacher some years later I learned that such a quest was common for almost all the adolescents I taught.

This book is concerned with the centrality of the body in contemporary adolescents' lives. If you take the experiences of my own school friends as commonplace, questions must be asked about the social circumstances that create these pressures and make parents feel they must spend thousands on orthodontic and dermatological treatments for their children. Questions must be asked about the social realities that cause children to feel that dieting or exercise or vomiting or even staring at their navels are all legitimate activities to enable them to feel validated about their bodies.

Teenagers are often seen to be concerned primarily with having fun. Robert Elms suggests that everyone wants a part in this fun and consequently 'nobody is a teenager any more because everybody is' (cited in Chambers, 1987: 2). Interest in pleasure is more important to most youth than interest in more serious activities (Reimer, 1995b:135). However, even perceived leisure activities can be serious activities for adolescents who feel self-discomfort. Take clothes shopping for instance. 'Our consciousness of dress is heightened when something is out of place' such as clothes not fitting us (Entwistle, 2003: 133). It can evoke a sense of discomfort and serves to acutely heighten bodily consciousness. For Craik, 'clothes are activated by the wearing of them' (1994: 16), thus it is the body which wears them that is of most importance. The physical body which lies under clothes, tattoos, piercings etc. is the focus of this book. It is this which impacts upon all other forms of bodily adornment and expression.

In most cultures throughout history the physical body has been viewed as essential for individual prosperity. In de-traditionalised times, people take individual responsibility for attaining such prosperity. Identity is often less predetermined for youths today. Perhaps family, neighbourhood and friendship even contradict the individual mobility and the mobile individual required by the labour market (Beck, 1992:88). Individuals in our modern western context are encouraged to live their own desired lives. 'Young people ... are able to choose more independently how they want to live' (Reimer, 1995b:122). They are asked to challenge limitations on personal freedom, starting with the basic power of appropriating their own bodies (Turner, T., 1994:28). Teenagers thus learn that it is legitimate to spend this independent time inspecting their navel piercing or assessing the progress of their teeth straightening. Indeed, success often demands spending time on such self-inspection and self-assessment. Late capitalism demands not just a hard-working person but one who exhibits the public characteristics 'of being an acceptable shape, size and 'well dressed', and who, therefore, confirms the desirability of the products of a service-sector economy' (Evans, 2003:10). The presentation of an acceptable body is almost essential for social validation, so the quest for body validation becomes a labour intensive but necessary journey. This book focuses on the social systems that school adolescents on the value of searching for body validation.

Talking to adolescents

The research on which this book is based was conducted across five second-level schools, in the greater Dublin area. The schools differed in ethos, denomination and student population. Two were private schools with a single-sex cohort (one boys' and one girls' school). One was a single-sex boys' voluntary secondary school. Another was a designated disadvantaged single-sex girls' school and the fifth a large co-educational community college.

I sought permission to talk to one first year class (approximately 13 years of age) and one transition year class (approximately 16 years of age) in each school. This meant that the sample was varied in terms of age. Students were introduced to the study and assured of confidentiality and anonymity. In total 242 teenagers were asked to fill out open-ended question and answer sheets. Questions concerned areas relating to diet, exercise and personal perceptions of their own bodies. The students were asked to indicate whether they would like to participate further in the study through in-depth interviews and to give their reasons why. On the basis of their responses and desire to participate further, fifteen girls and fifteen boys were selected for interview. Some were chosen because they indicated dissatisfaction with their bodies and others because they were satisfied. Parental permission was obtained before interviews commenced.

Each youth was interviewed twice, giving a total of 60 interviews. Most were an hour long and were conducted in the schools during school hours. I wanted them to feel free to talk about any aspects of their embodied experiences they wished and in whatever way they wished. Many of them had a strong sense that their views, behaviour and use of colloquial language was frowned upon by adults. It was important to react to their stories in non-judgemental, accepting ways in order to build their trust. I was acutely aware of the possible impact uncontrollable variables such as my own age and even physical appearance had on their willingness to disclose information. The teenagers indicated that they felt that the younger teachers were more in tune with their outlooks and lifestyles. I was conscious that my physical appearance might impinge on how freely participants would talk about issues such as fatness and thinness depending on how they positioned me as well as themselves within this spectrum.

Although I gave the teenagers had a good deal of freedom to direct conversations on the body as they wished, I also wanted to tease out specific areas of influence such as the media, the home, school and other social networks. I encouraged focus and interaction during interviews by means of visual images. At one point participants were asked to examine a silhouette outlining various body shapes and I asked them to rank those shapes in relation to their own shape and in relation to what they thought was an ideal body shape. At another point I asked them to look through a popular teenage magazine and identify what they liked and disliked about the bodies they saw. Looking at bodies proved to be a wonderful way of stimulating thought and discussion about them.

The focus of the book

The book questions how adolescents are schooled on or informed about the body. From the ever-abounding, ever-astounding body images portrayed in the popular press to the hushed comments directed at the bodies of school peers; from the popularity of those with the physical prowess to make it onto prestigious school teams to the influences of the physical regulation adopted by mothers and fathers, adolescents are schooled on the body. Combining academic theories and teenage narratives allows us to see how popular press, peers and parents influence teenagers' bodily perceptions and to what degree. Essentially this book provides a vital window into the worlds of the participating youths and, importantly, how they experience these worlds as embodied individuals. It offers much more than a dialogue with the social systems that educate teenagers, placing dialogue with real adolescents at its core. Rather than attempting to speak for adolescents, it provides a platform from which their own voices can be heard.

It became clear from interviews that peers schooled these teenagers on the body much more powerfully than did popular press or parents. The amount of discussion dedicated to each is intended to reflect this fact.

Chapter One brings the reader into the social worlds and personal narratives of the participating youths and focuses on how they negotiate the images they receive from popular press. Only certain types of bodies have been validated by popular press and advertising down through the years. The teenagers clearly negotiate their own relationship with the bodies they see. They point to the impact of media images on their perceptions of their own bodies. However, they appear never to be totally dominated by the media's portrayal of supposed ideal discourses. Rather, they negotiate which elements of these ideals will be personally enabling within their own peer contexts.

Chapter Two explores how popular press and peers police teenagers' bodies. Within a peer context this policing takes on a gendered dimension. The girls constantly talk about validation of the body and their approximation to it, to the point where it acts as a form of constant surveillance of bodies. Conversely, open body talk is completely rejected by these boys. However, it would be a mistake to presume that this allows boys to escape such social surveillance. On the contrary, the boys also police each other's bodies through physical displays of strength.

Chapter Three shows the important role the body plays in achieving peer acceptance during adolescence. The athletic body and the highly physical activities associated with it are particularly valuable. The boys involved appear to be highly dependent on participation in certain activities for forming friendships. Maximum body validation and recognition is attained through specific sporting activities in each school. To obtain and retain their places in such sports the boys are often schooled to push their bodies to a worrying degree. The body is also essential for obtaining and retaining places within romantic relationships. They seem to require what is considered to be a validated body form for acceptance and by virtue of being accepted, their bodies are further validated.

Chapter Four reveals the role and frequency of body stigmatisation in the lives of these youths and the calculated process by which it takes place. It seems that any perceived inadequacy can lead to an individual being stigmatised and that labelling focuses enormously on the body. Youths appear to have received an abundance of schooling on the stigmatisation of the underweight, and particularly the overweight, body. The chapter examines the emotional affects of body stigmatisation. It explores the complex strategies adolescents use to protect themselves against stigmatisation and its potentially crippling consequences.

Chapter Five focuses on the contradictions faced by teenagers to self-indulge yet self-regulate. The participants point to food as fulfilling valid desires, as well as being a source of self-sufficiency, independence and sociality. However, adolescents are also educated in the knowledge that body validation does not come from careless indulging. The respondents described strategies they use to counteract the dangers of over-indulgence. Unacceptable indulgence brings feelings of guilty eating, whatever the youths' sex or class. Some of the counteracting strategies they describe are worrying and even more disturbing is how common-place such strategies are in their narratives.

Chapter Six takes an in-depth look at working out, exercising and weight training, as an example of a counteracting activity. They view working out as highly validating; a view clearly perpetuated by the attitudes and practices of their parents. I show how these youths are schooled on the validating nature of regulation from peers, siblings, parents, and at the gym. This may be viewed as a process of social induction within validating activities. Many of the teenagers are schooled on the techniques of working out at the gym. They show how 'working on' the body or simply 'working' the body has the power to offer both body validation and embodied validation.

Finally, the key findings of the book are drawn together. They show how body validation and embodied validation is determined and measured and raise important questions relating to these adolescents' lack of formal schooling on the body within educational curricula and how this may be impacting upon their seemingly endless pursuit of validation.

1
Validated Bodies

Introduction

There are biological and social reasons why adolescents may be particularly susceptible to the powers and promises of popular press and advertising. Most adolescents are intensely aware of their changing bodies during their teenage years. Biological growth alters pubescent bodies where new outer contours and inner sensations, new physical pains and privileges emerge, making bodily self-consciousness common. And the popular press serves to enhance self-consciousness through encouraging individual deliberation upon the 'reflexive project' of the self (Giddens, 1991). Teenagers are surrounded by messages detailing what their physical self-project should exhibit in contemporary times.

Capitalist marketing and production knowingly homes in on adolescents' reflexivity upon their own bodies. Reflection on the body is likely to begin even before the teenage years. Quinion refers to a category of 'tweenagers' (children aged from 7 to 11) who are more street-wise, fashion conscious and media informed than in previous epochs. They have grown up through a period of economic boom and are fairly affluent. They live in small families with dual earners, with sizable disposable incomes. These tweenagers know how to draw upon strategies such as pester power to get what they want and are intensely aware of labels, media and technology (Quinion (2001) cited in Boden, 2006:291). Even the age category of 'tween-ness' itself has an inextricable link to the marketplace (Cook and Kaiser, 2004:204). By the time tweenagers become teenagers, they are usually highly self-reflexive. Not only have they had ample time to perfect the tactic of pester power but they may well have their own disposable income to buy into popular images.

Most teenagers have some form of disposable income, whether from employers or parents. Generally adolescents participate in the some type of part-time work. In Ireland 60 per cent of Leaving Certificate students have regular part-time employment. Students from less advantaged backgrounds are more likely to work, yet the purpose for which the finance is intended has become largely classless in that it is aimed at funding a 'lifestyle' rather than arising out of financial need (McCoy and Smyth, 2005). If lifestyle is to be projected through the self, consuming body images that are upheld and validated within popular press becomes increasingly important. These images are created by others and marketed aggressively and seductively (Tomlinson, 1990:13).

This 'suggests that within consumer culture a new relationship between the body and the self has developed' (Featherstone, 1991a:187). This new relationship could be characterised by an accepted obsession with bodily projection and perfection (Baudrillard, 1998:143). The consumption of images offers apparent control over the perfection and direction of self-identity. But the nature of consumerism is that the desire to consume must never end. It guarantees capitalist producers maximum control through advertising.

> It is not a question of the market reacting to the expressed desires – the sovereign needs – of the consumer, it is rather that the manufacturers deliberately attempt to shape consumer behaviour through advertising. (Corrigan, 1997:19)

This implies total dictatorship by the production sector (Baudrillard, 1998: 38). This is not to say that "needs are the fruits of production', but that the system of needs is the product of the system of production' (Baudrillard, 1998: 74). The market feeds on the inadequacies it generates (Bauman, 1989:189). Alarmingly, people run the risk of becoming engulfed in a merry-go-round of self-reflection and need for self-perfection.

Theories around the power of the press and consumption paint a picture of adolescents as passive receptors of meaning, whose bodies become slaves to capitalist messages. This chapter explores what adolescents see as validated body images, how they negotiate the images they are being schooled on and whether they become enslaved to the power of these images.

How the popular press validates bodies

The work of Foucault can help us understand how the press, media and advertising validate certain bodies and communicate this message to teenagers. They assign a status of truth to certain body shapes and sizes and promise increased fulfilment once individuals attain this truth. Foucault believes that individuals have always been searching for the promise of truth (1980): it is 'the ceaseless drive to establish normalizing regimes of truth that is characteristic of modern society' (McNay, 1994: 105). According to Foucault:

> Truth is a thing of this world: it is produced only by virtue of multiple forms of constraint, and it induces regular effects of power. Each society has its regime, its 'general politics' of truth: that is, the types of discourse which it accepts and makes function as truth. (Foucault, 1980:131)

There has always been an array of authorities which are considered competent enough to speak the truth. These authorities have effectively dominated populations and the individual bodies within them (termed by Foucault as 'bio-power' (1980)). They promise that the attainment of the truth they advocate will improve life for individuals and groups. In the past authorities such as the Church advocated that ultimate truth was to be found in Christian asceticism. With the rise of Industrialisation and Protestantism, such authorities claimed that maximum production and efficiency lead to the truth. In more secularised times authorities such as the media and press school populations on which regimes of truth they should normalise in their lives.

For Foucault truth is communicated through 'discourses'. Discourses communicate knowledge on regimes that should be processed and practiced within space and time. For example, monks in Christian monasteries described discourses of asceticism as the route to ultimate truth. The body has always been the focus of discourse and 'is not only given meaning by discourse, but is wholly constituted by discourse' (Shilling, 1993:74). The body is ultimately the main object of discourse, as it is the body which discourse targets and transforms. Similarly, within popular press and consumer culture, 'there is one object finer, more precious and more dazzling than any other ... That object is the BODY' (Baudrillard, 1998:129). I wanted to find out from the adolescents in this study whether popular discourses played such a powerful role in validating certain body images and if there was some ultimate truth associated with attaining a certain body.

How adolescents see the role of popular press

All thirty teenagers talked about how they are schooled on body images through advertising, magazines, television, models, sports stars, actors and singers. They spoke of how they are bombarded with images and messages that validate the thin body and good looks.

> Magazines, looking at models and film stars and people like that. I'd have loads of magazines and I'm always looking at them. (Chloe, 13)

> It's the media. Even if you're on a bus and there's an advertisement on a bus, and it's a girl, she's going to be skinny, like perfectly skinny. You never see anorexics or anything overly skinny but you see people who are just skinny enough. (Shauna, 16)

> In all the shopping centres and in the ads everywhere it's always good-looking people you see. (Rob, 16)

> Magazines, TV, music videos, the radio; even talking about new diets. Every-where it's just bombarding you from day to day. It's drummed into us every-day that we need to be skinny, like diet magazines. It's somewhere back there drummed into you that you should look like that. (Gillian, 16)

The adolescents felt that the press and advertising continually inform them about what a validated body looks like.

However there was no sense that this had occurred behind the backs of docile teenagers. They were acutely aware of why certain images are validated by the press while others are castigated. They knew that 'good looking' and 'skinny' bodies are used in advertising to increase the profit margins and publicity of certain companies and artists.

> They'd have to be models to be on an ad or else no one would want to buy what they're selling. It's because they're skinny, they wouldn't put big people on their ad or they wouldn't make money. (Eve, 13)

> Naturally you're going to see sexy, good-looking people on TV and in shop windows or else they wouldn't make any money. Nobody would want to buy the product if the models were big fat people. (Mark, 12)

> Celebrities get loads of money out of saying they have a new diet or whatever. (Anna, 16)

Magazines and famous people get publicity. (Kevin, 13)

Adolescents were fully aware of why certain bodies are validated within popular press and others relegated to the periphery. They frequently described how the omnipresent nature of certain body types in the press was a constant reminder of the status of truth and validation associated with those bodies. However, validation by external discourses was only one side of the process of validation as they described it. Teenagers themselves were also responsible for validating bodies in their local contexts.

How teenagers validate bodies

Popular press continually educates its consumers on body image. However if we presume that people imitate these images unquestioningly there is a danger of regarding bodies as passive abstracted, homogenised and objectified, as simplified and denied human agency (Monaghan, 2007:68). The teenagers' narratives indicated that they themselves must be seen to participate in a more complex way in producing validated bodies than common understandings suggest.

> The common social scientific reading of bodies as objects of a process of social construction is now widely inadequate. Bodies are involved more actively, more intimately, and more intrinsically in social processes than theory has usually allowed. Bodies participate in social action by delineating courses of social conduct – the body is a participant in generating social practice. (Connell, 2005b:851)

This sense of agency brings to mind Bourdieu's structuring habitus and Giddens' structuration theory. These theories propose that consumers of images retain their agency because if it was not for their individual consumption practices, production would cease to be.

Bourdieu's notion of *habitus* provides a valuable conceptual tool when applied to adolescents' own validation of certain body types. For instance, it reveals adolescents consuming social structures, such as images in the press, which in turn construct a habitus that organises body 'practices and representations' (Bourdieu, 1990:53). Such practices and representations can be 'objectively 'regulated' and 'regular' without being in any way the product of obedience to rules' (*ibid*), as Foucault might suggest. Practices undertaken to attain a validated body form are not viewed as com-

13

pliance with the rules but as empowering adolescents in their daily inter-action and communication.

The body with most interactive and communicative powers is, for Bourdieu, likely to have been that which was victorious in the 'field'. The 'field' is a type of 'competitive marketplace in which various kinds of capital (economic, cultural, social, symbolic) are employed and deployed' (Ritzer, 1992:542). Certain forms of capital achieve symbolic victory over others and therefore hold a superior status. On the surface, Bourdieu's notion of symbolic capital bears striking resemblance to Foucault's notion of dominant discourses of truth. However, their implications for adolescents as agents who validate certain bodies are quite different. Essentially, Bourdieu recognises that power is located 'in' and 'on' the body, rather than simply 'over' it. It allows the body to be a signifier of power as well as a receptor of power.

While Foucault has been criticised for examining the body as an 'object', Giddens has been criticised for falling into the trap of objectivism in his examination of the body as 'project' (1991). The body as 'project' appears to eradicate the corporeality of the body as it becomes an object that can be manipulated. Similar to Foucault's body, discourses have 'an im-mediate hold upon it; they invest it, mark it, train it, torture it' (Foucault, 1977:25-26). Unlike Foucault's body, however, this is a 'reflexive project' (Giddens, 1991) and any efforts to alter the body are explained by the pursuit of agency rather than the fulfilment of discourse.

If we only view structure as 'something which constrains action, or even determines it', we neglect the fact that, as Giddens argues, 'it is also enabling, it makes possible for us to do things' (Craib, 1992:34). One example of an enabling action is 'speech' (Giddens, 1976). Here Giddens draws on Goffman's 'shared vocabularies of body idiom' (1963a, 1967). Speech is an action which takes place within a structured framework of 'language'. However, language only exists in so far as people speak it and people only speak it because they see it as enabling to their everyday communication (Giddens, 1976). Similarly, adolescents are schooled on the body through discourses and they may use all, or perhaps some, elements of this schooling for purposes of enabling and empowering. What Giddens contributes to understanding adolescents' relationship with popular press is that the press provides a language in which the validated bodies can be decoded and understood. Adolescents must appropriate this language within their everyday actions, however, before it can be meaningful, enabling, empowering and crucially validated in social interaction.

Teenagers' role in validating bodies

The body images the youths preferred were those validated in the popular press (toned, thin etc). But the negotiation and assignment of a status of validation among the teenagers themselves happened within interactive settings such as secondary schools. The boys I spoke with largely felt that a fit and muscular body was validated for men in the press. Within their interactive school settings however, this body took on an enabling quality. The fit and muscular body was enabling for peer acceptance, for sexual attractiveness and for protection against physical domination (each of these areas is explored in later chapters). It was validated in their localised setting for its ability to enable these realities.

Those with muscular bodies were validated because this enabled them to get onto desirable school teams.

> I like a rectangular shape. Muscular on top with big shoulders. Tall enough and not too skinny ... Not fat or not thin but in between ... The lads on the senior cup team in this school would be built kind of like that, that's why they got picked. (Kevin, 13)

For others the muscular body was validated among peers because it enables strength, sexual attractiveness and acceptance.

> Muscular, you have to be strong and have a muscular body. For me it's to impress girls ... most fellas would be concerned about having muscles. (Mark, 12)

> Broad shoulders, strong chest, not fat thighs but big enough thighs. If you're not overweight and you're not underweight, if you're just the right shape and stature for your height, you're perfect ... Everyone would want to be with you. You'll have loads of friends both, fellas and girls because part of it is for girls. (Evan, 13)

> The burly look it's really what you want, you know like broad shoulders. They'd want to be thin, like have a thin stomach with muscles and biceps but they wouldn't want huge legs. It's kind of all about definition ... They [his peers] go to training and I know that some of them would deliberately do more laps

15

than others in order to get that. They'd do press-ups in their own time ... they're always measuring strengths. Girls like strong guys too. (Daniel, 13)

Muscles say to the girls 'oh look at me, I work out' and it makes the guy proud because he can show off his body more and not be 'oh I don't have muscles'. It'd be great going to the beach with a few friends and a girl and the others wouldn't want to show off their bodies without any muscles, but the guy could go 'yeah look at this'. When you have muscles you can get a bit cocky and say 'you can't stamp on me' and it puts other guys down. That's what I've noticed, if one guy has muscles, they put down other guys who don't have muscles. (Eoin, 13)

Many boys referred to the enabling powers of muscles in warding off any threatening advances while also encouraging more pleasant advances from the opposite sex. Some, however, were more concerned with enabling the former than the latter.

Being strong, you have to be strong. You can't be weak or be able to be thrown around. The popular people wouldn't be bullies but they would never be slagged obviously because they're popular. They'd be well able to handle themselves. (Andy, 16)

Some observed how the muscular shape reduced the risk of being slagged by peers.

Guys have to be tall, kind of 'muscley', you know bigger. It's like girls like to be slimmer but boys like to be bigger, 'muscley', bulkier. No one wants to be really thin or really big, they just want to be in between, just a bit 'muscley' and bulkier. Basically tall, 'muscley' with a six-pack ... They don't want to be too big and they don't want to be too small. They might get slagged either way. They might get slagged if they're big and they might get slagged if they are stick thin ... Most guys my age don't want big muscle but they're trying to get tight muscle. (Ger, 13)

All the boys agreed that muscles and athleticism are enabling and validated on that basis but could not agree whether broad shoulders are part of the validated physique. The desirability of broad shoulders depended on the interactive needs within particular school settings. The boys who attended a school where rugby was the most popular sport identified broad shoulders as vital for body validation. In the schools where Gaelic football and soccer were the most popular sports, 'definition' was important – but not the 'burly' look.

In general, good muscle definition was a common criterion for body validation among all the boys, but the degree of muscle required related to survival and success within specific social settings. The muscular and athletic body was validated not because it had such status within popular press but it was seen as a practical solution to complex problems and validated because it enabled the boys to overcome these problems.

The girls also validated the body type advocated by popular press, but did so because it increased their agency. Like the boys, the girls associated body size and shape with social positioning and levels of attractiveness. A thin yet curvy and toned body was validated most, because of its enabling qualities.

> I think thin is best. Yeah thin, have a nice smile, nice features on her face. A bit curvy because fellas like curves [laughs]. Everyone associates you with the weight of the group you're with. Like say if you were with someone that was fat or else someone that was real skinny, they'd put you into positions in it, like 'she's in between' or 'she's smaller than her' but you'd want to be skinny. Most girls my age are about a 6 or an 8. (Chloe, 13)

Here social positioning was dependent upon weight. Surely this also implies much competition for superior positioning within the group since most of its members took between size 6 and 8 in clothes. Others believed that being thin determined their position within same sex groups as well as determining how attractive they were to the opposite sex. Molly perceived herself as outside of her social peer group because of her size.

> I'd say any colour hair as long as it suits you. It doesn't really matter what colour eyes. Kind of thin and probably about medium height, not too tall and not too small. Long legs and little feet. Boys don't like girls that are overweight … In adult sizes most of my friends would be a size 6. It depends on the label because 8 is quite skinny in some shops. In ladies I'd probably be a 12 or a 14 so I don't really fit in with the others in terms of size. (Molly, 13)

Many of the girls described the validated body in terms of clothes size although the boys did not. Boys were more likely to relate size preferences to height. For the girls preferences in clothes size remained steadfast regardless of height. There was a three-year age gap between the girls I talked to, and a significant difference in height, but the sizes validated among both age groups were generally the same.

For the older girls too the skinny and toned body enhanced the possibility of peer acceptance and social admiration.

> I like the shape that they don't have really big boobs but they're okay and they're skinny but not too skinny and a really toned stomach. With the skinny ones you always see people looking at them enviously all the time as if they want to be like them and people who are any bit over what is considered right are kind of ignored. (Shauna, 16)

Social admiration in turn enhanced self-satisfaction.

> Probably not too thin and not too fat is the best, because you don't want them too thin like with their bones sticking out and all. You'd like a bit of weight on a girl. A bit of weight in the legs and stomach but definitely to be toned as well. My stomach, because I do dancing, it's toned. People say it to me as well and that makes me feel happy. You wouldn't want big saggy arms or anything but just to be normal. Like most people I know are just normal, about a size 8 or 10. (Caoimhe, 16)

The type of duality discussed by Bourdieu and Giddens was evident in most of the narratives. Firstly, the teens were schooled on the fact that certain bodies are validated within the press and its associated discourses. Secondly, they learned that certain bodies are validated because they are enabling to individual pursuits. As these conversations unfolded, a particular body shape emerged time and time again; the thin, toned body. It was the body most frequently validated within popular press and the physique most commonly identified as enabling.

The body validated by popular press

We have seen that both boys and girls validated bodies that emphasised western society's 'fascination with slimness' (Baudrillard, 1998:141). The continuous reproduction and re-emergence of the slender body image in the press point to its constant accreditation with the status of truth. Baudrillard describes late modernity's perception of the true body by the terms 'phryneism' and 'athleticism'.

> Phryneism being defined roughly as the woman of *Elle* and the fashion magazines, masculine athleticism finding its wider model in the athleticism of the executive, a model presented everywhere in advertising, films, mass literature: bright eyed, broad shouldered, lithe muscles and a sports car. This athletic model also encompasses sexual athleticism. (1998:136)

If we understand 'phryneism' to mean beautiful and charming, and 'athleticism' to mean defined and toned, we can see that Baudrillard's terms fit with the body so often described by the adolescents. Throughout the book this validated form is referred to as the 'aesthetic-athletic' body.

The aesthetic-athletic female body in popular press

In the west in the past, the plump and voluptuous shape conveyed physical expectations of femininity. The growth of consumer culture, the press and advertising in the 1920s saw popular depictions of the female body significantly slimmed down. Ironically, a more shapely and curvaceous body form returned to prominence in the 1930s and 1940s, the exact time when social circumstances of war more naturally facilitated the opposite. In the 1960s fashion models and entertainment stars again changed the direction of body size, down to Twiggy in the 1970s. Continuing in the 1980s, the thin body plummeted to levels of virtual malnourishment in the 1990s and has since wavered between this and a more toned look. There is no doubt that the slim body has retained a Foucauldian-like status of truth into the twenty first century.

We have seen many instances where famous women have been ridiculed by the press for becoming too thin. The validated body sits within a narrow margin. Never so muscular as to run the risk of looking masculine, this body generally boasts a significant chest size, thin waist, firm abdomen, pert yet understated buttocks, toned thighs and long slender legs. It is aesthetic and athletic. It is the true body of Hollywood; of the rich, successful and sexually attractive. This is the body which women of all ages speak of aspiring to.

> The contemporary popular media is saturated in images of thin and healthy beautiful female bodies. Female film stars, pop stars, cat-walk models, television hosts, the 'leading lady' of romantic fiction narrative, and advertising hoardings, in the main, operate under a 'tyranny of slenderness' (Chernin, 1983), where thin is beautiful, desirable, and valuable (transferring success onto a range of life goals, practices and products, and women who fit the thin ideal). (Redmond, 2003:172)

It is impossible for girls to escape the fit female body ideal or to escape reflection upon the validated status it depicts. According to Redmond, magazines are full of information on, and examples of, how real women have defeated their bulges and bulk and are thus placed alongside images of major and minor celebrities, making their positive, glamorous and ideal images appear the obvious indicators of femininity (2003:182). Images of celebrities such as Christina Aguilera, Girls Aloud, Renée Zellweger, Cameron Diaz, Nicole Richie, Angelina Jolie and Paris Hilton, among others, bombard magazines, films, TV screens, billboards, music stores and the Internet. They school global populations on a similar image of femininity, simultaneously making women incessantly aware of their deviation from it (Bartky, 1990; McRobbie, 1991; Bordo, 1993; Davis, 1995; Grogan, 1999 and Frost, 2005). It is common for celebrities to present their ideally proportioned, semi-naked bodies as an intrinsic and normal part of the rise to fame. These women are strong, secure and self-assured, possessing all the values young girls aspire to. Women such as Angelina Jolie and Victoria Beckham prove to admiring onlookers that is it not just in songs and the movies that the trimmed-down, toned-up body offers power and prosperity, but also in matters of love. Their bodies must be viewed as personifying beauty and attractiveness since men such as Brad Pitt and David Beckham, themselves icons of masculine perfection, have fallen for them.

An abundance of companies use the semi-naked, aesthetic-athletic body as their selling mechanism. These often portray poised moments of passion between an equally perfect man and woman: the man depicted as completely engulfed in the moment – in her beauty, in her body. The woman, although similarly lustful, generally keeps her eyes half open and stares into the camera. Her fit and firm borders mirror equality with his. Her desire, yet evident self-management, displays to others a true femininity. With her firm buttocks, flat stomach and half exposed breasts she often stands over him in a position of dominance. She is 'the 'new woman', unconstrained by biology or old social roles' (Bordo, 1994:293).

The aesthetic-athletic male body in popular press
A muscular male body has prevailed throughout history, although the degree of muscularity varies at different periods. Long before women's bodies became the focus of nude paintings in the 1800s, men with wide shoulders and tight buttocks were regularly displayed. It was not until the 1980s, however, that this semi-naked male body re-emerged as commonplace once again. The arrival of the Chippendales and the Dreamboys,

playing to exclusively female audiences, challenged the traditional boundaries between men as viewers and women as the viewed (Grogan, 1999: 17). Nowadays, the appearance of men's bodies in the press and advertising is aimed at schooling men on validated forms of masculinity more than it is at arousing women.

> While the reasons for it are contested, there is widespread agreement that a significant change has occurred, in which men's bodies as bodies have gone from near invisibility to hypervisibility in the course of a decade ... More fundamentally, there have been suggestions that males may increasingly be defining themselves through their bodies. (Gill, Henwood and McLean, 2005:39)

Whether selling aftershave, hair gel or jeans – and much else – most companies address a target male audience in their advertising. Most of today's advertisements have moved away from the earlier clean-cut look and display men with ruffled hair, dark eyes, rugged stubble and a perfect smile. He may be seen with arms positioned on his firm waist, leaving onlookers helpless but to be drawn to his muscular abs, broad shoulders, distinctive pecs and an abdomen that exhibits the definite outline of a six-pack. Not so muscular as to intimidate, his body is aesthetic, athletic and hugely desirable. Grogan is of the belief that:

> Adolescents present a slender, muscular ideal that is very similar to that of the adult male ideal. They are fearful of becoming fat, and would diet or exercise to avoid becoming overweight. Men are socialised from a young age to aspire to the masculine, mesomorphic shape, which is linked with concepts of fitness and health. (1999:127)

Muscles, therefore, are extremely important to masculinity. This study has already referred to boys' affirmation of the socially enabling qualities of the muscular body. Muscles have the ability to signify strong willpower and self-management. They proclaim an indisputable validation of maleness and manhood. Companies such as Marks and Spencers and Nike use the athletic, muscular body of footballer David Beckham to market their products and Beckham is now as well known for his body as he is for his football skills. Once a symbol of the working class, muscles are now synonymous with a classless masculinity. They are the essence of male validation and acceptability. Whether it's pop stars like Justin Timberlake or rappers like Eminem sporting his Calvin Kleins, 'their shirtlessness is intended as sincerity, their exposed muscularity as dignity in labour'

(Fussell, 1994:54). This laboured self does not indicate the body of a working class labourer as it may have in the past, but rather of modern labour in the form of planned training and workouts. Celebrities globally display the fruits of a self-styled modern-man's labour. From Terminator to Gladiator, the aesthetic-athletic body is constantly gazing down from billboards and TV screens.

Men's bodies have become subjected to a process of aestheticisation not previously witnessed. Men's bodies are now targeted in the press and advertising for purposes of aestheticisation, as long since done for women (Baker, 1994). Companies had to find a way of 'persuading men that it's actually macho to use a moisturiser' and not feminine to have a facial, 'hence the pictures of hunks splashing on the perfume' (Baker, 1994:132). There is even suggestion that it is now possible for heterosexual men to appropriate 'bits and pieces' of homosexual styles and practices (Demetriou, 2001), which has given rise to the notion of the 'metrosexual'. The metrosexual man is but one among a number of recent labels which have attempted to depict a type of 'new man-ism', such as the new lad, millennium man, the dad lad and the colditz man (Beynon, 2002:119).

The aesthetic-athletic body has emerged with a status of truth and has been validated within popular press but the process by which the teenagers report that they negotiate this truth is extremely interesting.

Adolescents as negotiators of body images

To make any suggestion that adolescents negotiate discourses of truth affords them some level of agency. This would seem to be appropriate given that they have indicated that the quest for an aesthetic-athletic shape is about more than adherence to external dominance. It is because this physique is expressive and enabling in social situations. This view recognises growing boys and girls as active creators of their own lives – both individually and collectively (Connell, 2005a:13). They are not just passively engaged in role learning and being 'socialised' (*ibid*).

In many ways adolescents do not simply conform to structurally imposed discourses, but negotiate them on the basis of how they can be used for enabling purposes. There is a distinct individualised, decision-making process which is negotiated on the journey from discourse to practice. This notion of individual negotiation of body images has been addressed by Monaghan in relation to bodybuilding and more recently obesity. He holds that 'clearly each bodybuilder is an individual ... participation does not entail a transitory loss of self or individuality' (1999:275). Similarly, he suggests that overweight people 'are not passive McDonalized dopes, just as their bodies could not be standardized like one Big Mac' (2007:89). But empirical research, which allows us to understand how individuals negotiate body discourses in relation to their own embodied needs, is overwhelmingly absent.

> Many writers lament the fact that the increasing theoretical interest in the body has not been accompanied by empirical studies (e.g. Davis, 1997; Wacquant, 1995; Watson, 2000) ...The sociology of the body has, by and large, ignored the voices that emanate from bodies themselves. (Gill, Henwood and McLean, 2005:40-41)

It is vital that the journey from discourse to practice lend itself to individual diversity. According to the adolescents in this study, the process of negotiating discourses of truth is highly complex and subjective. There was no straightforward acceptance of a single aesthetic-athletic body with identical definition, dimensions etc. Definition and dimensions were negotiated in light of the expressive needs of each teenager. Through dialogue and deliberation they negotiated how they should personally interpret the images they received from popular press. This process gives a far more individualised and dialectical element to the Foucauldian journey from discourse to practice. It shows that the journey from internalising a body image such as the aesthetic-athletic body, to participating in practices to attain it, is quite subjective and discriminatory.

How the aesthetic-athletic body is negotiated by adolescents

I asked the teenagers to select the celebrities they thought to have the best body shape from a popular magazine. This magazine was selected randomly but like all other such magazines or forms of popular press it contained an abundance of images of stars and models. The aesthetic-athletic body form was evident throughout. However, while the teenagers could see this common body form, they also focused on individual differences between bodies and attached significant meaning to these differences. Deciding on the celebrity with the best body shape required active negotiation and individual reflexivity. They participated in a dialogue with the self when negotiating the images. Their answers often highlighted the role of human subjectivity within this process.

> Maybe someone like that [Duncan from former boy-band 'Blue'] because he's not too muscley. Maybe her for a girl [model in advertisement] because she looks friendly and she's not too skinny and she's not too overweight. You can't really find the perfect person because everything varies really. (Darren, 12)

Some rejected the particular bodies that others thought were the best. For instance, Barry thought Beckham was too thin.

> Not David Beckham, he's a bit thin. Ben Afflick is probably the best because he's not too small and he'd be well built. (Barry, 16)

Others preferred David Beckham's body but still rejected elements of his image.

> Ben Afflick he's big, he's huge, too big. Obviously David Beckham because he's a soccer player he has to be big. I know a lot of girls go for Justin Timberlake, he's skinny but he's not too skinny. Fellas themselves don't want the long hair David Beckham look. They don't say it but they obviously want to be him because he's one of the best soccer players in the world. Even though they think he's a bit gay. (Andy, 16)

The teens partook in a dialogue with the images presented to them, making the internalisation of discourse a complex, lengthy, reflexive and discriminatory process. David Beckham and his groomed look may cause him to be described as a metrosexual male in contemporary times. For many of these youths however, the metrosexual must display overt heterosexuality. Rather than being free to experiment with 'bits and pieces of homosexual styles' (Demetriou, 2001), these young boys seemed to be locally quite restricted in their experimentation. Ging's Irish study also found that:

> Limited versions of the masculine (in school, family and community life) may... restrict young men's ability to explore and enjoy the diversity of images of and discourses on masculinity that are becoming available in the media. (2005:47)

Men's conversations about their bodily appearance are structured by a narrow range of key discourses (Gill, Henwood and McLean, 2005:43). Popular press may validate particular images of men's bodies but these were only validated in the adolescents' local settings if they remained within the boundaries of the dominant (heterosexual) masculinity. This pervaded the discourses defining gender identity for all of the boys. A definite sense of homophobia was present in the way the boys accepted or rejected body images (similar to that found in studies by Mac an Ghaill (1994), Lynch and Lodge (2002) and Norman *et al* (2006)).

Many of the boys emphasised the importance of displaying an empowered heterosexuality and physical dominance because they were advantageous for everyday survival.

> I don't like David Beckham, he's too much of a ponce with the pony-tail and wearing skirts. They're all around 5'10 or 5'11 and they're not really fat or skinny. I'd say Jonny Wilkinson or Ben Afflick are the best, they're the right shape. They have broad shoulders and they look strong. You'll always want to be strong and muscles make you look kind of tough and like you have a strong arm if you wanted to hit someone. You wouldn't want to fight but if someone wanted to fight you, looking so strong might put them off. Girls would want a fella that's big and strong too. (Josh, 13)

When the boys evaluated the men's bodies in the magazine, they did so on the basis of what having this body would mean in everyday life. They tried to gauge whether it would be enabling in their local settings or validated by peers. For example, Josh discussed why he preferred some men's bodies over others. His decision related back to what a particular body would enable 'Josh' to do in everyday life. Eve was one of the girls who also did this.

> Jenny out of 'Atomic Kitten' she's nice looking, all of them are but she's lovely. She has a lovely figure, but then she's probably on loads of diets or something but she is lovely looking and has a lovely figure. Now I wouldn't wear any of them [tight top, short skirt]. Too short, my mam would kill me. I wouldn't wear anything like that because I have loads of brothers and I'd be scarlet. I'd like to have her figure but I wouldn't like to have my hair like that. (Eve, 13)

While Eve liked what the celebrity wore, she knew this image would not lead to validation for her personally in her daily interactions. As we have seen in the conversations, there were two sides to body validation. Bodies were validated by popular press but they were also validated in localised adolescent settings, not because of adherence to messages from the press but because they were locally enabling. So adolescents do not adopt and internalise 'the practices that signify and articulate discourses in mechanical or fully predictable ways (Butler, 1997, p.19) but discursively (re)configure, (re) form and (re)shape these in different ways into personal modes of being' (Halse, Honey and Boughtwood, 2007:223).

Adolescents' critiques of the popular press message

What Foucault neglects is the process by which individuals negotiate discourses of truth. Foucault's journey from discourses of truth, to making them functional practices in life is short and straightforward, whereas these youths validated truth only when they had negotiated its enabling implications. Equally, they were never so enthralled by the bodies validated in the press that they could not identify what they perceived as flaws in these images. They thought that some celebrities looked good at times, but did not like them at others.

> Victoria Beckham has a gorgeous figure. Although sometimes she can be too thin but other times she's nice. (Anna, 16)

> I like Britney for her body ... She has a good body, but then I think her face can look like a man's sometimes. (Cian, 16)

The adolescents continued to focus on the importance of having a trim, toned shape but also felt that these celebrities put in an unrealistic amount of time and enhancement.

> Britney has a great shape but she has people working on her all the time and as my mam says she's been working on that for a long time. (Chloe, 13)

> Britney just has a nice shape, even though I know she's probably dieted hard or even had surgery on it. (Evan, 13)

> David Beckham has a good shape but so much work goes into him and there's camera effects as well that it's unrealistic at the same time. (Brian, 16)

> I think Victoria Beckham has a gorgeous figure. She wears fabulous clothes ... But then I do look at her and say to myself if I had all that makeup and all the effort put into me I'd look gorgeous as well. Like I think they're still the same people as us it's just that they have people going around putting makeup on them all the time and top range clothes and have all the money to get like facials all the time. (Lynn, 16)

The participants often mentioned the role of the press in schooling them on validated body images but they were well aware of the inaccuracies in this information.

These teenagers were certainly influenced by celebrity bodies (Bartly, 1990; McRobbie, 1991; Bordo, 1993; Davis, 1995; Grogan, 1999 and Frost, 2005), but through their individual negotiation and interpretation, refutation and adaptation of such bodies, they displayed active agency rather than cultural complacency. If we ignore how teenagers negotiate discourse in relation to their own unique expressive needs, our understanding of their embodied selves is 'reduced to an effect of image consumption' (Budgeon, 2003:42). It would result in a singular interpretation of teenagers as media complacent, while 'the process and practices through which the self and the body become meaningful are left untheorised' (*ibid*). Discourses of truth may exist within a structural realm of the press but negotiating truth needs to be both theoretically and empirically viewed as an individual process of empowerment. Discourses are 'taken up and incorporated into subjectivity in different ways and to different effects' (Halse, Honey and Boughtwood, 2007:231). Even though an aesthetic-athletic type body is validated by popular press, every body in advertising is essentially different, just as every adolescent body is different. The attainment of body validation during adolescence is not about mirroring a predetermined image. Rather, it comes from the negotiation of this image by each adolescent to enable their own expressive needs within differing interactive contexts.

Conclusion

The introduction to this chapter suggested that emerging biological changes and social roles can cause adolescence to be a time of immense reflexivity upon body image. Advertising and the press serve to increase this reflexivity, given the financial gains which are to be made from schooling individuals on the notion that they are somehow lacking. Certain body forms are validated through their omnipresence in the press, media and consumer culture. This may have been viewed by Foucault as popular press producing body discourses which hold a status of truth. While the adolescents concurred with this reality, they were also acutely aware of the financial motives that drive displays of bodies in the press.

Adolescents also pointed to a dualism within the validation of certain bodies which both Bourdieu and Giddens' theories acknowledge. Here the body is validated by the press and by adolescents themselves through their localised interactions. Importantly, a particular body image is not validated simply because it adheres to structurally imposed discourses, but because these discourses present adolescents with enabling possibilities. Hence, the body is validated because it is enabling to individual social pursuits on a localised level.

The body most referred to by these youths took the form of what I call the aesthetic-athletic body. It is beautiful and charming, trim and toned. This is the body form that appears to dominate ideals of masculinity and femininity in popular press. However, its negotiation by adolescents was by no means generalisable. The body type was negotiated by these adolescents in a very individualised manner. The youths negotiated the information they received on the body from the press and then decided which elements should be adapted or rejected for their own bodily displays and pursuits. They also identified falsehoods within supposed discourses of truth, making their journeys from discourse to practice decidedly reflexive and discriminatory.

2

Policed Bodies

Introduction

With the emergence of new physical contours and sexual drives, adolescents are likely to be particularly vulnerable to displays of gender and a need for gender validation. The body is vital here, in that gender is constantly validated through visual physicality. The body is indicative of culture and choice, and embodied projection is a personal way of taking up and reinterpreting received gender norms (Butler, 1987:133-134). Popular press produces discourses educating individuals on how bodies should be received and read; particularly 'gendered' bodies. For Bordo 'no body can escape either the imprint of culture or its gendered meanings' (1990:109). The notion of gender as something which is visually interpreted may unquestionably cause adolescents to be more conscious of their external appearances, bodily presentation and 'the look' (Featherstone, 1991a:179). After all, masculinities and femininities are formed in a process of social embodiment, in which bodies, and also social relations, are shaped (Connell, 2002).

Both the boys and girls identified how the press and media validate an aesthetic-athletic type body form, as Chapter One showed. Many commentators (Bartky, 1990; Baudrillard, 1998; Bordo, 1993; Corrigan, 1997, Foucault, 1977, 1979, 1980; Giddens, 1991; Shilling, 1993, Turner, B., 1984, 1992, 1996) have discussed how the constant display of supposed validated bodies in the press and advertising causes individuals to self-scrutinise and self-criticise their gendered projection. These images may be seen to police bodies by reminding people of their approximation to or deviation from the accepted body forms. But validation of the body also takes place in localised, and inevitably gendered, peer interactions.

Since peer interactions play such a vital part in sanctioning validation, this chapter explores how adolescents police and evaluate each others' bodies. The data causes us to question whether too much emphasis has been placed on the role of the press in policing bodies and not enough on the role of adolescents themselves in this process. The narratives demonstrate the level of policing that adolescents partake in to negotiate the assignment of validation. They also emphasise the degree to which policing the body takes distinctively gendered paths.

How bodies are policed

The work of Foucault offers insight into how the body emerges as an entity that is policed in modern times. Popular press and advertising certainly act as discourses that school individuals to varying degrees on bodies that hold a status of truth but they may also be seen to act as a form of surveillance that polices the implementation of truth through its constant presentation of discourses. This occurs in a way similar to the way prisons in the nineteenth century used a Panopticon, a central watchtower designed so the entire prison could be observed at any time. Prisoners became permanently aware of an authoritarian gaze focused upon them and regulated their behaviour accordingly. Through such surveillance, regulation took place through 'progressively finer channels, gaining access to individuals themselves, to their bodies, their gestures and all their daily actions' (Foucault, 1980:151). Rather than inflicting pain on the body to control the prisoners, as previously, the Panopticon generated greater and more effective control. Prisoners began to police their own bodies with 'disciplinary technologies' (Foucault, 1977), driven by consciousness of being watched. This type of surveillance also became common in wider society (Foucault, 1979).

When older forms of bodily control such as torture or public spectacle began to disappear, control began to operate through internalisation and to a large degree became self-surveillance (Wolff, 1990:125). While adolescents today may be free from the gaze of prison officers, the power of particular discourses can leave them feeling they have a societal gaze fixed upon them, constantly scrutinising any failure in their implementation of such discourses. According to Bartky, in the constant self-surveillance of the 'inmate lies the genesis of the celebrated 'individualism' and heightened self-consciousness which are hallmarks of modern times' (1990:65). If bodies that hold a status of truth are validated throughout magazines, newspapers, television, billboards, department stores, music, film, the internet and all forms of press and media, we can come to feel haunted by our own deviation from this truth. To view the press and advertising as such a policing force fits with Corrigan's notion that:

> We are always being scrutinized, we are always being evaluated, our very being is absorbed into the ways in which others look at us: at every moment and in every way we may fail the test of the scrutinizing world. (Corrigan, 1997: 68)

Chapter One pointed to the omnipresence of an aesthetic-athletic type body in popular press. This could be construed as a scrutinising presence over adolescents, yet they maintained a notable agency in their negotiation of this body type. Although there was a sense of being looked upon and perhaps scrutinised by discourses of ideal bodies, adolescents were equally looking back at and scrutinising such bodies. The data indicated that adolescents felt stronger about the role of their peers in scrutinising bodies because it was ultimately within the peer context that real validation was sanctioned. Policing, therefore, seems to be less top down surveillance from dominant discourses and more horizontal surveillance from peers. And this peer policing happens within a definite gendered framework.

Girls policing girls' bodies

There appeared to be a distinctly gendered dynamic to the way adolescents policed each other's bodies and assigned a status of validation to certain individuals. The girls constantly talked about who in the press or among their peers had a 'good' or 'nice' body. These conversations acted as surveillance: through their endless talk about which peers projected a validated body and even which elements of any one body should be validated, the girls relentlessly schooled one another on the assignment of validation. The pursuit of validation was a central part of their everyday communication and this made the girls aware that their bodies were under continuous surveillance from other girls. To put it in a Foucauldian framework, it was not the guards who policed the prisoners from a panoptic vantage point. It was more the prisoners – or in this case the adolescents – who policed each other through visual surveillance and incessant oral dialogue.

Almost all the girls described discussions at school about body image as commonplace and pervasive. The pursuit of body validation from peers was an issue that was raised time and time again. Scrutinising one another in order to assign validation happened on a daily basis in their school environments.

> Girls never stop talking about what people look like. It's the one thing that's always a topic of conversation. Whether someone's lost weight or put on weight. Whether someone's too thin or too fat. (Shauna, 16)

> Even when you go out, it's all 'what's she wearing and does it look nice and does she have the figure for that?' They'd be always saying 'she looks too fat in that or she looks too skinny' or if the colours didn't match. (Anna, 16)

> In class it'd be 'oh she's after loosing loads of weight or she's after putting loads of weight on' ... Every day there's like a comment about someone. Even if it's their hair or something about their appearance anyway. (Lynn, 16)

> I know this girl in the year and she'd see a girl and say 'oh my God she's put on so much weight, did you not notice she's put on weight?' And I guess that's one of the bad things about being in a girls' school, they're very bitchy. Like they'd talk about you behind you're back ... like it's a huge thing and girls make it out to be such a big thing. They're always like 'oh my God I've put on weight I have to go on a diet'. (Sarah, 16)

> I got put in the front row now for talking about my weight [laughs] and my friend that sits beside me ... And my other friend that I used to sit beside. Girls are always on about weight. (Eve, 13)

The girls indicated the extent to which they inform each other on whether and how to modify their bodies. They continuously negotiated modifications via dialogue with friends. They accepted without question that girls talked about weight 'all the time'.

These girls constantly evaluated each other's approximation to validated body forms through open dialogue. Many discussed their perception of their own approximation to acceptable body forms or their sense of deviation from them. Most talked quite freely, but also critically, about their physical characteristics.

> I have strawberry blond hair, I have blue eyes, I have a chubby face. I'm a bit overweight and medium height. (Molly, 13)

> I'm not too tall, not too small, just the right height. I have blond hair and blue eyes. I'm not fat. I'm thin in the stomach like but I've fat on my arms a little bit. My arms are big like. (Caoimhe, 16)

Some were definite about changes they would like to make to their bodies in order to feel more validated.

> Well there are things that I'd like to do to make myself better...like I want to tone my stomach but don't want to go on a diet. I'm not exactly the fittest person in PE or anything like that. (Shannon, 14)

> I don't think I'm gorgeous, massive. I don't think there's anything good looking about me, but sometimes I do get a bit of confidence. I do think I'm fat sometimes and say I'm going on a diet. Sometimes I feel comfortable but other times I don't. (Anna, 16)

The girls frequently discussed with their friends whether they were happy or not about their bodies, whereas the boys were schooled on the body in a way that did not allow them openly to negotiate the assignment of validation to one another or to express concerns about their bodies.

Boys don't talk about their bodies

The majority of the boys I spoke to feared rejection from friends if they talked about their bodies in the same way girls did. The gender dynamic among the boys gave rise to a complex situation where they feared rejection from peers on the basis of being labelled 'gay' or 'girlie' if they talked about how they or other boys looked. The narratives purported an interplay of maleness that called for 'having a laugh' and 'not taking yourself too seriously' (Gill, Henwood and McLean, 2005:54).

This unwillingness to talk about issues of concern corroborates the findings of other studies. Cleary found that 'research now shows that men's and women's needs and inputs around friendship are not dissimilar' (2005:166). However, men have particular problems around same-sex friendships due to a traditional male schooling in displays of self-sufficiency where 'any kind of confessional disclosure would likely be rejected by other men' (2005:167). According to Ging, the adolescent boys who participated in her study were well aware of the dialogic differences between men and women when it came to discussing emotions. The boys involved perceived

> ...women as more mature, more complex, more emotional and better at dealing with problems than men on account of their ability to talk. Men, on the other hand, were often described as insecure, immature and unable to show their emotions. (Ging, 2005:40)

When asked to describe themselves physically in general terms, five of the boys remarked that they had never been asked such a question before. After long silences, they provided answers loaded with unfamiliarity and unease regarding talk about the body. Answering proved to be quite a difficult task.

> It's a hard one, I don't really know. (Andy, 16)

> No one has ever asked me to describe myself, so I'm not really sure. (Barry, 16)

> I wouldn't have a natural way of describing myself. I've never been asked that question before. (Ger, 13)

Other boys gave almost identical responses.

Although the girls might never have been asked such a question directly before either, their flowing and immediate responses evidenced a fluency surrounding body talk. Girls replied instantly, with descriptive and often critical observations about their bodies.

According to all fifteen boys, guys rarely talk about concerns relating to physical appearance or about physical appearance in general unless it relates to slagging other boys or to the exercise and training regimes of other boys (both of which I return to later). It seemed to be an unwritten rule that they would not discuss body image or any associated worries amongst each other.

> Boys never talk about their feelings, no. They talk about TV, girls, sport or something that happened the day before. It's just those four topics. (Evan, 13)

> Guys would never say 'I'm after putting on weight'. (Brian, 16)

> No never. You'd never say 'oh I have a savage pair of pecks coming on' [laughs]. (Enda, 16)

For some it was laughable even to imagine boys discussing body image with their peers. One stated that doing so would just make them seem vain.

> No never [laughs]. Unless they were real vain or something. (Kevin, 13)

The gendered dynamics surrounding body talk which these boys accepted, implied that they were not supposed to pay too much attention to the way they looked. While they were certainly expected to care about it, they were not expected to talk about it, least of all express concerns about it.

> You'd never talk about your weight. We'd never talk about it, never, ever. (Andy, 16)

> I've never actually had a discussion with a guy over his appearance or anything. (Cathal, 16)

> None of my friends have ever mentioned anything about the way they look or feel about themselves. (Ger, 13)

Ger did not think this was because they were all happy with their bodies. He indicated what he felt lay behind the silence.

> No I'd say it's because they think it's macho not to say anything. They don't want to be girlie and talk about being overweight or being underweight. I wouldn't personally talk about stuff like that with my friends. We wouldn't mention it to anybody. (Ger, 13)

The boys certainly had concerns regarding their weight, but would never tell their friends. Boys would just not talk about anything that would make them seem vulnerable or sensitive (i.e. 'girlie').

> When I thought I was fat I kept it to myself. Didn't really see it as any of their [friends'] business. Usually I just keep stuff like that to myself. I'd say most fellas are like that but yet they care. Guys don't really talk to each other about stuff like that. (Barry, 16)

Many of the boys told me there were elements of their bodies they were unhappy with, yet they rarely if ever talked to other boys about such matters. Even though the boys did not discuss bodily concerns, it would be a mistake to think this meant they had none – a mistake which many commentators have made.

Do boys care about their bodies?

Existing research resonates with mine, suggesting that girls frequently criticise their bodies and express concerns about their appearance. Perhaps there is a perception that boys do not need research to investigate their bodily concerns because they seldom refer to having any. Yet these boys' stories indicate that we should not assume that adolescent boys have no bodily concerns but fear the peer rejection which might result from revealing such concerns. Boys' apparent unwillingness to express emotions has been called a 'male crisis' (Connell, 2005a:11; Connell, 2005b:840; Beynon, 2002:75). Beynon asserts that this crisis has been enhanced by the evolving structure of work, where women are seen breaking through glass ceilings. He believes that where there has been a rise in feminist movements, men's emotional illiteracy, suicide rates, health problems, shorter life expectancy, underachievement in school and overrepresentation in crime have all risen (cited in Haywood, Popoviciu and Mac an Ghaill, 2005:195). Although bodily concerns do not feature on this list, masculinities must be understood as embodied and the interweaving of embodiment and social context among young men must be addressed (Connell, 2005b:851).

Feminists have long been advocating that women are most frequently targeted by body image discourse in the press. This is in spite of the emergence of a vast array of images of men as we saw in Chapter One. Feminists suggest that feelings of bodily inadequacies are women's issues. Frost refers to research by Fombonne (1995); Ransley (1999); Favazza (1998); House *et al* (1999); Philips (1996) and Grogan (1999) to assert that all describe body dysmorphia and dissatisfaction as being predominantly women's concerns. After all, girls 'expressing dislike of their bodies is common' (Frost, 2005:64). She goes so far as to suggest that having recognised that as...

> women are of course the most clearly trapped in the narcissistic, self-surveillance world of images' (Featherstone, 1991:179), it may be that there is a tendency to theoretically underestimate the extent to which relations between body and self are gender specific. (2005:71)

Grogan, Connor and Johnson maintain that measures of body dissatisfaction are greater in heterosexual women and homosexual men, than in heterosexual men (2004:505). They believe that homosexual men are under more pressure than heterosexual men to attain an attractive (slim and muscular) body (*ibid*:507). However, given that emerging research (Cleary, 2005; Ging, 2005; Gill, Henwood and McLean, 2005) stresses a general reluctance among men, particularly heterosexual men, to express any emotional concerns, it may be that their level of bodily concerns has been underestimated. Many of the boys I talked to wanted to distance themselves from body talk because it was associated with being 'girlie' or 'gay'. This indicates that it is more accepted and expected for heterosexual women and homosexual men to talk about their bodies, but it does not mean that all heterosexual men are satisfied with their bodies. Neither does it mean that they are under less pressure to attain an attractive shape, simply that it is unacceptable to talk about it. As Morgan suggests:

> Just as it would be wrong to accept uncritically the idea that women are the more embodied gender, so it would be misleading to see men straightforwardly more embodied than women. (1993:71)

When asked to evaluate their bodies in non-verbal ways, the boys were more critical of their bodies than the girls. All youths were given a silhouette of body sizes ranging from one to nine. The first body in the range was numbered One, and showed a skinny frame, while the last body in the range numbered Nine, displayed a significantly overweight image. The adolescents were asked to identify the shape they thought to be ideal and the image they felt their own shape was closest to. The results produced gender related data which were somewhat unexpected.

Significantly, four of the fifteen boys and four of the fifteen girls chosen to participate in this study were hand picked on the basis of expressing contentment with their physique. The reality turned out to be quite different. During our discussions, all thirty participants made some reference to body dissatisfaction or a desire for self-alteration and many of the eight chosen for their self-contentment turned out to be the least satisfied of all. Once again, their expression of dissatisfaction revealed a strong gendered dynamic.

It has been suggested that the girls policed each other's bodies through their incessant, descriptive and vivid discussions on body validation and concerns about their perceived deviation from validated forms. This vocal, social dialogue has led to a view that girls are more concerned than boys with body image. However when these girls were asked to identify the silhouette shape they thought was most ideal and the one they were closest to, seven girls noted their self-image and the ideal image (number three) as the same number on the range.

Out of the fifteen boys interviewed, only two equated their own image with what they believed was the ideal image. With image number four being the most commonly identified ideal, many rated themselves either overweight or underweight in comparison. If this numerical rather than discursive form of self-evaluation, albeit in a limited sample, is to be taken as accurate, it suggests a worrying and largely unexplored relationship between boys and their bodies.

Boys policing boys' bodies

The girls I spoke to certainly policed each other's bodies and their own through constant visual and verbal scrutiny. This activity also provided a form of schooling on the assignment of a superior or inferior status to certain bodies. There are complex meanings attached to what 'woman express through their talk about their bodies' (Blood, 2005:45). Through linguistic expressiveness, women use the language of the body to accomplish the meaning and collective interpretation of their utterances within their specific peer context (Potter and Wetherell, 1987 cited in Blood, 2005:61). If using language expressively is so important to the construction of meaning, then two questions arise with regard to the boys I talked to. Did they fail to construct meaning surrounding their bodies? This is unlikely. Or did the male interplay which caused verbal limitations in expression lead to different modes of construction?

The boys' construction of meaning about bodies and the policing of bodies took place through physical activities rather than verbal dialogue. This fits with Cleary's findings that 'men don't reveal problems because this is not behaviour that is associated with being a man'; revealing difficulties is associated with weakness, whereas the performance of masculinity is about strength (2005:160). The young men in Ging's study also reflected this process of emotional suppression and physical expression. She notes that:

> While participants were often critical of the constraints imposed on boys to suppress emotion and act hard, they also seemed to derive considerable pleasure from the performance of tough, blokish masculinity. (2005:41)

Kehily and Nayak make a similar point about the importance of how boys are schooled on macho masculinity, within a playground game of 'punch-'n-run' (1997:137). They suggest that such games create male cultures where 'macho' lads are seen as 'proper' boys (*ibid*) or given a validated status on the basis of their superior physicality. These blokish performance techniques 'as stylised and enacted through the body, enable boys to position themselves as clearly identifiable heterosexual masculine subjects' (Dalley-Trim, 2007:201). A dominant form of masculinity is validated through shows of strength and policed through shows of strength, while emotionally weak boys risk being rejected. Proof of masculinity depends upon the steady confirmation of power (Segal, 2007:104).

These boys negotiated who was to attain body validation in a way that resembled Foucault's (1977) description of pre-panoptic surveillance. It was done through physical force and strength. Challenging and tussling with one another seemed to be an inevitable aspect of the boys' assigned physical status. Without a body of strength and pace they lost out in such wrestling and scuffling. They policed each others' bodies through physical challenges, using brute force to distinguish who had a body worthy of validation from who had not. Dalley-Trim similarly found that the boys in her study used physical dominance to police forms of masculinity.

> Their 'power,' in terms of the dominance assumed by and afforded to them was blatantly obvious in their interactions with other members of their respective class: interactions saw them police their fellow class members, specifically the masculinity of their male peers, and saw all others rendered silent and marginal. (2007:213)

Here, physical strength is essential for the validation of masculinity and the validation of the body.

The boys talked about how their peers constantly competed with one another in measuring their strength. Although validation of the body was not discussed among the boys, it was certainly demanded.

> They're always measuring strengths. (Daniel, 13)

> Physical messing just happens with all the boys. (Josh, 13)

Some spoke of the need to be aware of their own physical capabilities should they be approached and challenged. The boys policed their own and their peers' bodies to gauge how successful they might be in these school yard contests; to gauge whether or not they would be physically validated amongst their peers.

You might get knocked down...you'd be always aware of it. (Evan, 13)

It's all about pushing each other and pulling and holding each other in headlocks and stuff like that. You'd need to be able to hold your own. (Enda, 16)

We stand around talking about TV and sport and pushing into each other messing ... It would be just pushing them and then getting them to chase you, it wouldn't be that physical but then I'm not weak myself. I'm not small for my age so it's natural for me to be strong. The smaller fellas would be weaker. (Kevin, 13)

The use of brute force produced a distinctive type of reflexivity. The boys constantly reflected on how a strong and athletic body was required to defend oneself.

I want to know I can defend myself. Like if someone pushed me up against the wall I want to know that I can push them back. If I'm weak then I'm not going to be confident doing that and then I just wouldn't be happy with myself. (Rob, 16)

It was largely bodies that were successful within such active contests that were awarded a status of validation. The need to police the body for the purposes of negotiating and assigning validation was not so different among the boys and girls I spoke with. Rather, it was the expression of this policing that was highly gendered and differentiated.

Conclusion

Much sociological literature on the impact of popular press on teenagers' relationships with their bodies has emphasised the meaning of this relationship in the construction of a gendered identity. The press might be seen to heighten adolescents' awareness of their deviation from validated interpretations of gender. This chapter, however, highlights the importance of more localised relationships with peers in policing the body and schooling each other on validation. More importantly we have seen how girls and boys police and school each other in distinctly gendered ways.

It would seem that girls participate in relentless visual surveillance and verbal commentary about each others' bodies. Through such practices they negotiate how they should pursue and attain a status of validation, while constantly monitoring their own approximation to or from it. The picture seems quite different for boys, however, as they emphasised their reluctance to participate in dialogue on the body with each other, particularly with regard to bodily concerns. It is perhaps this gendered dynamic, where girls talk more openly about the body and bodily inadequacies, which has led to a presumption that boys are less concerned than girls about their bodies. But this chapter has shown that boys were afraid of being rejected by other boys if they expressed concerns about their appearance.

These boys did not police each other through talk of body validation, as this might be construed as feminine or weak. Nonetheless, they did police each other and negotiate the assignment of body validation in a macho and physical way. They indicated how physical contests and the policing of strength were normal within their school environments. Undoubtedly, engaging in practices that base acceptance on rejecting emotional expression and valorising physical expression perpetuates dangerous expectations of masculinity and exacerbates concerns about boys' modes of expression in general.

3

Accepted Bodies

Introduction

Adolescence is a time when youths begin to move away from dependence on their parents for acceptance and support towards dependence on their peers. As the time when movement is away from 'significant others' (parents) towards the 'generalised other' (peers) (Mead, 1934) adolescence is described as the stage of 'social redefinition' (Steinberg, 1996:103). Mead stresses the importance of the generalised other as being the way in which individuals begin to experience their own identity from the 'particular standpoints of other individual members of the same group, or from the general standpoint of the social group as a whole' to which they belong (1934:138).

But acceptance among peers is seldom a smooth process, particularly in the school context. For adolescents, 'schools are the most important formal institutions in their lives' (Connell, 2005a:21). Connell even suggests that 'the growth of a secondary education system was a key condition for the emergence of 'adolescence' as a social category' (*ibid*).

Adolescents appear to be divided into three distinct peer groups in the school system: formal, semiformal and informal (Rice, 1999). Membership within each group conveys a certain level of social status, achieved on the basis of desirability to become a member of that group. These subsystems provide a logical framework through which 'cultural capital' (Bourdieu, 1984) can be examined. Cultural capital exists in three forms: in an embodied form, expressed in one's self-presentation, vocal articulation and aesthetic practices; in an objectified form through cultural goods

43

such as art, media, literature, architecture and machines; and thirdly, in an institutional form through educational credentials (Bourdieu, 1984: 243). What Rice refers to as 'group status' (1999) among teenagers may be based on a mediation of some form of Bourdieu's cultural capital.

Chapter One examined how teenagers school one another on what a validated body looks like and Chapter Two discussed how adolescents and their peers police each others' bodies. It follows that during adolescence, acceptance within the type of peer subsystems Rice speaks of may be significantly tied to the body and displays of embodied capital. This chapter examines how embodied capital enables access to certain activities and social groups. Such access occurs in quite different ways for boys and girls and this chapter looks at some of the gendered differences in peer acceptance. It also examines how hierarchies and strategies of acceptance are played out within the formal school structure and, interestingly, how embodied capital is used by the youths to neutralise their displays of less favourable forms of cultural capital.

Boys neutralising academia through sport

In his division of peer subsystems within secondary schools, Rice holds that adolescents are involved firstly in a formal academic subsystem formed by school administration, faculty, curriculum, grades and rules. The students 'are concerned with intellectual pursuits, knowledge, achievement, and making the honour roll' (Rice, 1999:241). Adolescents who falter in their competitive academic pursuits or what Bourdieu might call institutional (educational) capital (1984) risk being excluded from this group. Equally, involvement may be damaging in schools where academically inclined students are rejected socially. This applies even more to boys if it is true that 'girls rate hard work as being important in contributing to academic success whereas boys rate cleverness, talent and luck' as claimed by Ireson and Hallam (2001:184). Gill, Henwood and McLean's study found that:

> Men were keen to distance themselves from being seen as too serious, too committed, too earnest – things that were likely to attract a comment about obsession. Being cool seemed to involve a stance of distance or disinterest. (2005:54)

Being seen to be overly concerned with the pursuit of institutional (educational) capital and associated academic tasks was a cause of significant unease among the boys who took part in this study. They claimed that too much attention to the academic demands of the school system could jeopardise their acceptance among peers – unless they could prove that they were also involved in highly physical embodied activities, or that their academic success was simply a result of 'natural' intelligence. It is difficult to be at once an 'academic achiever' and a 'macho lad' (Mac an Ghaill, 1994), so activities such as sport are used to strike a balance. This clearly gives rise to a reality whereby one form of cultural capital has the ability to neutralise another and suggests that this neutralisation is necessary for successful social validation.

One boy talked openly about how letting his commitment to academic achievement be apparent has left him disliked by his peers and how other boys avoid this by not displaying their academic ambitions publicly.

> I just know an awful lot of people who don't like me ... I know they don't particularly like me for different reasons. Maybe they don't like my attitude to schoolwork because I consider it to be serious. I do really try whereas some people don't really care about school and they should or maybe they do care but they don't want to let on. I'm not afraid to let on that I care about school because it is important, but some fellas are afraid to let on because it makes you 'uncool' to care about school. (Brian, 16)

Brian may have unravelled what lies at the core of educational capital for these boys. Maybe it was not about caring or not caring but about a 'display' of not caring. This concurs with the Gill, Henwood and McLean study, which found that 'having a laugh' and 'not taking yourself too seriously' are essential to masculinity within postmodernity (2005:54). It was the notion of display which made the boys' predicament so complex, since they knew that commitment to schoolwork was necessary in an individualised and competitive system, but that a display of such commitment was crippling. Displaying unacceptable immersion in academic work simply created an imbalance in what the boys were able to talk about and this could in turn lead to exclusion.

> People who study a lot, they don't have much of a social life so they don't have anything to talk about when they come into school except school work so they kind of have their own little group. (Rob, 16)

Teens discussed the need to display their dedication to popular activities such as sport and socialising if they were to achieve successful social validation and social popularity. Many boys who risked over-association with institutional capital neutralised this association through displays of embodied capital.

> If all they want to do is learn and study and do their homework then it's real hard to do anything with them. Whereas if they're just naturally smart and they like coming out socialising and doing sport then it's alright. (Kevin, 13)

> Some people who are very smart might not get involved in after school activities but just focus on school. Everyone knows they shouldn't take it that seriously. It's good not to let homework and schoolwork take over your day but to do other stuff as well. You should get involved in activities after school, like all your friends and then you'll become more popular, but if you don't do any sports after school and you're clever, then you probably won't be popular. (Josh, 13)

Neutralising institutional capital with embodied capital was not so essential for the girls. While no one wanted to be considered a 'nerd' or a 'swot', none of the girls indicated that strong involvement in formal subsystems would influence acceptance within peer groups. The only reference to this issue was made by Gillian, who displayed educational capital but did not feel the need to neutralise this with involvement in sport.

> Yeah I get on well academically but not in sport. It's either academic or sports, well you could be good at both but I'm not great at sport. (Gillian, 16)

It was acceptable for Gillian to have an overt interest in academia without needing to neutralise this by being equally involved in other activities. Within the formal or academic subsystems educational capital was interpreted and projected quite differently by the boys and the girls. Ownership of educational capital was expected by all, but the boys faced the predicament of how much they could safely display. Hard work was respected among girls, as Ireson and Hallam suggest (2001:184), and hard work may be respected among boys too – as long as they keep it to themselves or work equally hard at extracurricular activities.

Friendships based on sport
The ability to talk about and participate in sport did not only neutralise involvement in formal subsystems but also played a significant role in

acceptance within semiformal and informal subsystems. According to Rice (1999), semiformal subsystems involve participation in sports, drama and developmental clubs. Acceptance by peers in informal (friendship based) subsystems could be greatly affected by one's position within such clubs.

> The amount of prestige that any position bestows depends on its rank within each respective group and the prestige standing of the group in relation to all other groups. (Newman and Newman, 1987 cited in Rice, 1999:241)

All three forms of Bourdieu's cultural capital may be important for inclusion in semiformal and informal subsystems but these stories suggested that certain displays of institutional capital can be viewed as unfavourable for inclusion among teenage boys. Bourdieu describes objectified capital as cultural goods such as art, media, literature, architecture and machines (1984). These adolescents referred to objectified capital in the form of TV programmes, films, music technology and computer games and outlined how displays of such capital have positive implications for acceptance in semiformal and informal subsystems. In an objectified form of TV match coverage and sport related computer games, sport offered platforms of common interest on which many of the boys based and validated their friendships, although participation in physical training and games created even stronger platforms from which to launch and validate friendships.

Chapter Two suggested that the adolescents are socially schooled to communicate verbally in distinctly gendered ways: open and descriptive among girls and unsure and restricted among boys. This appeared to be confirmed by what the teenagers said about how they achieve peer recognition and acceptance. Some of the girls believed that their open methods of conversing made it easier to form friendships.

> We just talk about anything. Girls do talk a lot. We talk about life and what's out there for us. (Shauna, 16)

> I think boys aren't as close to each other as girls, they're always slagging each other. Girls slag too but I'd know what would really hurt them and I wouldn't say it. I think fellas have to work to fit in but I don't think girls do generally. They talk more openly and it makes them closer. They talk about boys and clothes and lots of things. It's just lots of chatting and messing around but you can't really explain what it is because certain people wouldn't get it. (Sandra, 13)

Sandra seemed to think it could be difficult for some people to under-stand exactly how girls bond with each other, but what is certain is that these girls did not place the same weight as their male counterparts on sharing common interests to construct friendship bonds. None of the girls insisted that mutual interests were essential for creating friendships, although many recognised how interests in similar semiformal activities could make friendships stronger and more durable. The boys, on the other hand, spoke of friendship groups being formed on the basis of mutual interest in various forms of cultural capital, and all made some reference to sporting interests.

> Everyone's interested in girls so that's one thing that everyone can come together with but there'd be lads that would be into rugby and lads that would be into skate boarding and they generally wouldn't mix. (Enda, 16)

> Like if you have something that you feel confident you want to talk to them about you just become a part of that group. Like sport or computer games. They just talk about things they have in common ... With my two friends they just enjoy doing the same things I enjoy doing. I don't really try with anyone else. I'll still talk to them but I wouldn't have much in common to talk to them about. (Barry, 16)

> The people who play chess in our class all hang round together, so do the people who play Gaelic and soccer and the people who play hurling hang round together and then there's like the people who have the same interests but they mightn't be other people's interests, they hang round together. Like those people who like the same TV programmes, who just have the same interests. (Mark, 12)

The idea was mooted that a friendship could not be validated if two people don't share similar interests. Participation in semiformal sub-systems, therefore, did much more than determine one's prestige within friendship groups as Rice suggests; they appeared to be a prerequisite among boys for entry into friendship groups.

> If someone likes tennis and someone else hates tennis but likes rugby and the other guy hates rugby then they're not going to be very good friends because they don't share the same interests. If you were talking to your friends and you're talking about rugby or tennis or whatever and the other guy wouldn't have a clue what's going on, he wouldn't fit in so he wouldn't be friends with them in case that conversation comes up. (Josh, 13)

Participation in a physical activity such as rugby could make a boy a valid member of a particular peer group.

> In this school, for example, if there was a whole group of fellas and they were friends before they started playing rugby but then they all started playing rugby and they were all good at it, then they'd have an extra thing to talk about and that person that didn't play rugby wouldn't be able to talk to them because he wouldn't know as much about it but then he'd just start playing it so that they'd notice him more and they'd be able to talk with him. (Kevin, 13)

Mutual displays of certain forms of cultural capital provided not only a geographical meeting place for these boys but also a conversational one. Whether meeting to watch sport or to play, sporting activities were a strong binding force.

It is little surprise that many of the boys cited maintenance of friendships as being one reason for taking part in sport and for their desire to continue to do so in the future.

> If I didn't play Gaelic or soccer I'd lose a lot of contacts. I don't play for that, it's to be fast and fit, but I would if I stopped playing I'd lose a lot of contacts because most of them play Gaelic and soccer. I'd definitely lose a good bit of contacts if I didn't play sports. (Ger, 13)

> It's fun and keeps me really fit. I don't want to give up any of them because I just enjoy them so much and I get along with everyone on the team as well ... Most of them on my team live a good bit away from me. If I gave it up I wouldn't get to see many other people from other classes. It just helps you socialise. There was this guy in my class who had no friends so he decided to take up a sport just so he could make some friends. (Evan, 13)

> I will always play sport and as well there's a really big social life to it, like most of my mates play a sport or like one. (Rob, 16)

The boys commented not only on its facilitation of friendships, but also the value of sport for shaping up a fast and fit body that enabled them to access some of the most prestigious positions in their schools.

Prestigious school activities

Their stories have indicated how boys use sporting activities to neutralise their studiousness and thus validate their social standing, and also to form, maintain and validate their friendships with peers. However, the level of validation they were accorded depended not just on involvement in sport *per se,* but also on having the body type which facilitated access to and was maintained by participation in the most prestigious activities.

Rice holds that sport, drama and clubs are all part of semiformal sub-systems in educational institutions (1999:243). If activities are based more on hierarchy than parity, however, adolescents may find negotiating which activities are most likely to lead to peer acceptance quite complex. Connell cites Foley's findings concerning the supremacy of those who played sports in rural Texas. This hierarchy was only among boys and indicated various types of masculinity:

> The sporting Anglo 'jocks', the anti-authoritarian Latino 'vatos', the complicit but inconspicuous 'silent majority'. The jocks hold most prestige, the vatos maintain a cool and ironic distance. (Connell, 2005a:21-22)

According to Foley and Connell, participation in athletic team sports is a primary form of validating masculinity. Swain's study of three British schools produced similar data showing the importance of embodied per-formances in sport for the validation of masculinity.

> For much of the time the boys defined their masculinity through action, and the most esteemed and prevalent resource that the boys drew on across all three schools to gain status was physicality/athleticism, which was inextricably linked to the body in the form of strength, power, skill, fitness and speed ... Sporting success was a key signifier of successful masculinity, and high performance in sport and games was generally the single most effective way of gaining popu-larity and status in the male peer group. (Swain, 2003:302)

The importance of specific sports for the validation of femininity is less prominent in educational and sociological literature. Probyn states: 'for me as for many other feminists, sport is a sociological area of which we rarely speak' (2000:14). The power of the press and policing peers leaves little doubt as to the value for girls of a trim and toned body, but its vali-dation was not connected to involvement in specific team sports in the same way as for boys.

The girls spoke of engaging in hockey, basketball, football, athletics, gym-nastics, dancing, aerobics and drama but did not prioritise one over another. It was the physical result of participation in activities that was important for peer validation, not the specific activity. They talked about the centrality of the body in peer recognition and popularity but had no need to participate in a particular activity in order to achieve a high status of body validation. Having an aesthetic-athletic body was their greatest concern, whereas for the boys athleticism afforded greater prestige when associated with specific activities. Boys pointed to a clear hierarchy of activities which lead to varying levels of validation among peers and how only particular physical activities influenced social standing.

> If you're on the soccer team here it's pretty big because if you're on the chess team who cares. Soccer is cool. (Mark, 12)

> Everyone wants to play soccer, then rugby, then Gaelic and so on. The chess people would probably be known to be like nerds. (Darren, 12)

> Football is probably the most obvious sport that people would want to be in, then Gaelic, hurling, maybe basketball and they're probably the main sports. There's table tennis and cross-country but they wouldn't be the same as football. (Cian, 16)

The highest social positions were reserved for those who had been re-cognised for their displays of athleticism and skill on the football pitch. An awareness of privileged access to resources is the motivation to achieve status and the motivation itself produces, and is produced by, social hier-archies (Marmot, 1994:90). The boys were well aware of the privileged access to resources enjoyed by youths who were good at sports such as soccer.

> In a boys' school you have to be good at sports. The popular guys are really good at soccer and stuff and are out playing on the Astroturf every day. (Mark, 12)

> Soccer is the highest. In terms of popularity you don't get higher. In my ex-perience when people have won in Gaelic and hurling it hasn't been as bene-ficial to them as winning in soccer has been. Soccer must be the cool thing to be involved in now because they see their idols in England playing for Man United and that, because we're getting to that age now that if they're going to make it then they're going to go to England in the next few years to play if they're good enough and if they go to England, they're going to be very popular when they come back. They'll be idolised. There are a few teams here in Dublin and if you play for them then you're going to be idolised as well. (Andy, 16)

Here, 'heroism is measured on the basis of displays of physical prowess and innate skill' (McSharry, 2008:95). The status of male sporting heroes confirms the prestige attached to competition and the competition for prestige. This makes sports such as football 'extraordinarily popular, with high rates of participation by adolescent boys' (Connell, 2005a:15). As a recreation involving bodies in ritualised combat, it is presented to 'enormous numbers of youth as a site of masculine camaraderie, a source of identity, an arena of competition for prestige, and a possible career' (*ibid*). The narratives endorse the notion that increased recognition and respect is invariably linked to highly physical team sports (Lynch and Lodge, 2002).

> If you're on the school sports teams you're going to get respect. (Cian, 16)

> People on the soccer teams are never slagged or anything like that. Nine times out of ten. I don't know maybe it's that you're scoring goals for the school. It's just popularity ... they're generally good at sport, grew up playing for the schools teams, winning games and scoring goals. (Andy, 16)

> Everyone knows you if you're on the main rugby team everyone respects you. In the older age groups you get away with a lot more things. Everyone would want to hang around with you ... The rugby teams are just regarded as better. They get away with a lot of things from teachers. Senior and Junior Cup teams would be regarded highly and in our year if you're on the As or the Bs. (Josh, 13)

> All the guys on the Senior Cup team are the popular ones because all the younger lads look up to them as heroes. The Senior Cup is so massive, every school ... wants to win it. We haven't won it in many years and that's not good considering the record this school used to have. There would be a lot of pressure to do well. (Enda, 16)

Greater respect was shown to members of soccer, rugby and Gaelic football school teams, all of which demand physical fitness and precision. But peers' respect and adoration is not assured (Bauman, 2005:50) and keeping their team places demanded dedication and determination.

The physical competition for acceptance

Masculinity formation now takes place almost as much on the sports field as it does in sexual encounters (Messner, 2002). For Boden:

> Sports, for example, according to Chung (2003), prizes traditional values such as hierarchy, patriarchy, male supremacy, heterosexuality and nationalism, and awards wealth and fame to those who have proven their athletic ability and can maintain their awarded status on and off the field. (2006:290)

Whatever the team sport, it is predominantly men's leagues and competitions that attract most media support and public interest, so physical team sports are largely gender specific and male orientated. Those who attain places on teams and exhibit practical strength and athleticism in their bodily actions and visual strength and athleticism in their bodily shape are likely to receive accolades from peers and rewards from teachers (Lynch and Lodge, 2002).

The girls I spoke to did not talk about the prestige of those on the girls' school teams and barely mentioned competition for team places. Several did acknowledge the need for fitness and endurance so they could perform well in individualised sports such as running and gymnastics. But sporting prowess hardly influenced their social standing at school, whereas for boys the football field was the site where validation of bodies took place in a legitimate framework. Because of the prestige attached to being on certain teams, a type of 'warfare' (Frank, 1991) was played out against opposition teams and against their own team members in the competition for places. While securing friendships might have been one reason why these youths participated in sport, friendship turned into combat on the pitch. Their attitude to competition within teams parallels Frank's 'dominating body', which seeks out other bodies as the enemy to fight and perpetuates the self in fighting and winning (1991). Frank asserts that this body needs to fight because it is only through fighting that proof becomes apparent of the self-worth of one and the self-lacking of another. These boys' outlook also echoes Messner's 'bodies as weapons' (2002), where the body becomes a vehicle for achieving victory within combat and competition:

> They do compete definitely in sport...In sport guys want to be better than each other the whole time. (Kevin, 13)

> In school, sport is really competitive so one always tries to be better that the other, to be captain or something. Boys want to be better than everyone else. (Darren 12)

> The older they get the more competitive they get. In soccer at this stage they're either trying their best to get to England or to get noticed by the better teams. They're really, really competitive. (Andy, 16)

> Rugby is hugely competitive because there's always someone who wants to take your place. For the lads on the seniors and juniors there's always a lad younger than them who wants to take their place on the team so they need to work at it and keep it up. (Enda, 16)

It is not only in competitive battles against opposing teams that status is decided, but within the team itself (McSharry, 2008:98). These boys were aware of this individualised competitiveness and had obviously been schooled on the expendable nature of the individual and their team place. This brings to mind the fluidity of modern relationships and contracts (Giddens, 1991; Sennot, 1994; Turner, B., 1999). Boys were alert to the instability of their places within popular activities and teams. Their uncertainty resonates with Giddens' 'pure relationships' (1991) in connection with the instability of marital relationships. Sennet's metaphor of the world as an airport departure lounge, where all relations are momentary and replaceable (1994), is perhaps more applicable. Nonetheless, such fluid and fleeting relationships inevitably come with postmodernity, because 'the postmodern world is one of shifting or thin solidarities and ironic or cool loyalties' (Turner, B., 1999:44). Much like these school teams, 'such a world is described sociologically by the development of the revisable self and negotiated community of temporary loyalties' (*ibid*). These adolescents pursued validation through places within prestigious team activities. But this pursuit was complex because should other commitments weaken their commitment to the group activity, they could immediately be replaced by another willing recruit.

The boys 'must continuously physically compete against their own comrades to maintain their position' (McSharry, 2008:98). They needed competitive drive if they wanted to retain their place in the group and continue to receive team recognition.

> You always want to be the best. It's just a drive you have in you. You have to have ambition ... In PE we do this run around every time, it's like six laps of the Astroturf and whoever does it first you get lined up and if you do it better it's better for your team and if you do it better for your team you get congratulated. It's a feel good feeling. (Mark, 12)

Those who didn't live up to the physical challenge of the team activity risked their peers' disapproval and even rejection.

> In sport even if your coach doesn't say you're not playing very well, your team mates are going to say, 'what's the story, what's wrong?'. If you had all your friends giving out you'd try to do your best. (Cian, 16)

> There's one guy and we're going on a cycling trip on Tuesday and he's massively overweight and he's got chronic asthma and everything and he's bringing down the group and we all think it. We can't go as fast because he won't put the effort in, it's not so much that he can't but he won't try....It just really annoys me. (Enda, 16)

> When I was in sixth class I got the ball and I was about to pass it to another guy. He ran into me, he rugby tackled me and he was on my team and he punched me in the stomach and then just got up, grabbed the ball and walked off. The other time we were playing indoor hurling here and one of the other guys charged at me and bashed me off the wall. I think they just don't like me being in a sporting atmosphere in the first place, they don't think I'm good enough. I'm small and not athletic. (Cathal, 16)

Some youths lacked the embodied capital required to receive the physical validation needed to make it onto school teams because they were too fat or too thin.

> Some people aren't agile enough to do the things that involve running or that. You'd need to be very fit and if you're really heavy and slow it won't help. (Josh, 13)

> There was this guy in my class ... he was very skinny. No one would pick him for sports. (Evan, 13)

Interestingly however, even those who felt they did not have the embodied capital to attain positions on school teams acknowledged the social status that was attached to such positions in the school system.

Those who felt that a place on prestigious teams was within their grasp were driven by a competitiveness that made them constantly afraid of being displaced and replaced.

> I always turn up to try to make an impression and to try to get into the next team. It's hard to get on sometimes but if a player who is in your position on the next team doesn't play well, you have to try and play well every week just in case he slips up one week and the coach might see you and put you up. (Josh, 13)

If physical team sports are viewed 'as a violent competition between teams of males seeking territorial power and control' (Langman, 2003: 223), displacement and replacement are unavoidable.

Team sports are complex and retain places for those who possess a particular type of energy, prowess, strength and athleticism. Swain found that bodily strength 'was a prerequisite in physical games that were deliberately designed by the boys to test toughness and stamina' (2003:304). This emphasis on physical competiveness fits precisely with the way boys policed each other's bodies and assigned a status of validation accordingly, as we saw in Chapter Two. The retention of team places and the associated prestige also depended on validation of certain bodies, and the boys were acutely aware of the need to push their bodies in order to retain such social positions. While few empirical accounts describe the lengths youths will go to for recognisable body validation, the narratives here reveal just how seriously some adolescents take the maximisation of their athletic abilities. Speaking of the recent death of a young rugby player, one boy hinted at the extremes youths might go to, to ensure the body validation needed to keep their team position.

> He was probably using enhancers like EPO and NESP which basically gets your heart rate up to a hamster's heart rate ... every sport uses them. (Enda, 16)

Self-discipline, dedication and physical drive were identified as essential for validation in sport. Individual training was taken on to improve fitness and thus ensure a place on a desired team.

> I try to go to training as much as I can and to matches as much as I can. I just go out and try, and try real hard, to get a lot better at the sport. (Kevin, 13)

> I'd have twelve or thirteen training sessions a week. I would go to all of them. (Evan, 13)

> I train, I play football, I go running in the park ... I work on it and work on it. I play hurling as well on Thursdays in school. I try to play lots of other sports and get my fitness up and just try and play better than the person I'm marking. (Ger, 13)

They pointed to the success and endurance of sports stars who attained body validation for the purpose of maintaining physical focus.

I always say to myself just keep going, look at Ronaldo and look at Beckham, they would have done the same thing. So 'just keep going you're nearly there' I always say to myself. And then just the though of how big they are and getting to their level ... and all the girls like the [laughs]. I'd say to be a big footballer, you'd actually have to be good looking. Like Beckham you see him in all the ads and posters. (Eoin, 13)

Here the aesthetic and athletic aspect of this embodied capital are both significant for body validation in semiformal activities. Both aspects were also extremely important for validation in informal or romantic activities.

Making a physical impression

The adolescents demonstrated the significance of attaining various levels of social acceptance through participation in particular activities. Social acceptance is vital in gaining recognition within peer and romantic relations. Rice holds that during adolescence 'informal subsystems' or 'friendship choices are directed overwhelmingly to other students in the same school, and ... to members of the same grade and sex group' (1999: 243). By the same token, romantic relations are intrinsic to the teenage years: the interplay between peer relations and romantic relations cannot be separated (Connell, 2005a: 17). 'Adolescence is the period in which heterosexual couples become a normative pattern in peer group life' (*ibid*). It appears that the normalisation and expectation of heterosexuality still applies. According to Haywood and Mac an Ghaill, educational institutions discriminate against those who do not normalise heterosexuality.

> In terms of sexuality, compulsory heterosexuality is used to characterise the ways that education arenas structurally discriminate against people with different sexual identities... Males and females, heterosexuals and gays/lesbians, exist in unequal structured oppositions. (Heywood and Mac an Ghaill, 1997:51)

In school settings the expected sexual preference is for the opposite sex, and these teenagers did not refute this. The romances they talked about were exclusively heterosexual. Youths were careful to distance themselves from any association with homosexual desires. As in Chapter Two, it was the boys who were keenest to disassociate themselves from any appearance of having 'gay' or 'girls" tendencies.

However, the teenagers revealed an intriguing distance between boys and girls and highlighted the importance of embodied capital in bridging this gap. They saw the unfamiliarity between boys and girls and believed this intensified the role the body played in the establishment of friendships and especially romantic relationships. Many of the respondents reported feeling uncomfortable around members of the opposite sex. It seems youths may still be coping with the consequences of the long tradition of segregated schooling in Ireland. When they came in contact with the opposite sex they tried to make an impression rather than build friendships. They described the body, rather than conversation, as most often used to speak a familiar language.

Most of the adolescents at single-sex schools said they would make more of an effort with their appearance if they went to a mixed school. They stressed the importance of being accepted as attractive and desirable. Interestingly, the older teenagers who had attended co-educational schools were better able to form genuine friendships with the opposite sex and less likely to feel the need to impress. The junior students in co-educational settings, however, described the same concern to make a good impression as those in single-sex schools. Adolescents in single-sex schools explained how they would try to perfect their bodies to allay anxiety over their appearance and make themselves attractive if they went to mixed sex schools.

> I'd be more concerned about the way I look. I'd want to do my hair different maybe and some people would probably put on makeup before they come in to look nicer. (Amy, 13)

> I definitely, definitely feel I would care more...I think if there were girls in the school you'd put more of an effort into your appearance. (Cian, 16)

Where informal mixed activities had been arranged, or even when there was only a chance of bumping into someone of the opposite sex, the teenagers described how they intensified their self-maintenance regimes.

> I'd say a lot of guys would try to show off if there are girls around and that. They'd probably make more of an effort with how they look. Any time the girls from Saint Bríd's are coming up to do the plays you'd see people making more of an effort. (Josh, 13)

Some of the lads would be dressed up to the nines and they're just going to school to do a few rehearsals, they're not going out. The girls put in a huge effort. They all wore their best, best clothes. (Andy, 16)

There's a youth place we can go to just to play sport and stuff and that's one of the main things because there's fellas there, I'd wear make up. (Sandra, 13)

I remember we were making the film in fourth year and one of the films was on lads and the lads came up to the school and the girls just freaked. They were like 'oh my God, my hair, my hair, my hair'. 'Has anyone got blusher, concealer?' Seriously like the lads were walking and there was a big group of girls following them. (Sarah, 16)

These teenagers believed that boys and girls being schooled separately created a complicated unfamiliarity and that this elevated the importance of the body for interaction.

In a mixed school you learn to get on better with fellas, make friends with them. If you're in a single-sex school you'd see a fella and think 'boyfriend'. You wouldn't get to know them as friends ... There are only girls in all girls schools and that can make them more desperate to get a fella because there's no fellas in the school. (Tara, 15)

I was in an all girls primary school, and wearing makeup and what way my hair was and how skinny I was didn't really matter to me...On my first day in a mixed school I remember putting on my makeup and doing my hair up and everything. My skirt was down to here [points to her lower shin] because you get a really long skirt and then after a few days I started rolling it up until it was above my knee and that was important to me, how short my skirt was or to open the top button of my uniform shirt. (Shannon, 14)

So an individual who displays aesthetic and athletic assets may not only gain access to prestigious positions, as we saw earlier, but can also communicate with others through impressive interaction rather than conversation.

The data suggest that if teenage boys and girls are unfamiliar with a socialisation process where inter-sex friendships are as natural as same-sex friendships, then any interaction is likely be based more on sexual attraction than friendship construction. These adolescents observed that in countries where schooling was mixed, youths were less likely to rely on their bodies for expressive purposes. From their experience of working with exchange students, some participants suggested that mixed schooling in central Europe produced people who were less bodily conscious or aesthetically focused.

> It seems in Ireland the only way you can make fella friends is if you know them from primary school or you meet them at discos, where you can't really talk, or they're friends of friends. There's nothing like in Germany where they have youth clubs and dance classes ... that was just the way it was so it was much easier for the girls to be around the fellas. When my exchange student came over here to an all girls school, 'the convent', it was such a shock to the system because she was used to sitting beside fellas in class, but there was just girls everywhere. Then when we were over in Germany some of my friends were going around wearing these tiny tops, trying to impress the guys, but the German girls just don't see the need. (Gillian, 16)

Students who had moved to Ireland from elsewhere noticed a difference in the interaction among boys and girls. Even in the co-educational schools some attended in Ireland, they noted how the adolescents saw each other in sexual as opposed to friendship terms. One boy from Australia noticed how nervous Irish girls were when he tried to talk to them. He seemed baffled by the extent to which the sexes kept themselves separate.

> In Australia you can talk to girls as if they were your best mates and over here I find it difficult because when you talk to girls they go a bit icky and a bit nervous. In Australia you'd call the girls tomboys because they hang round with the boys and over here it's different because I see the girls hanging around with the girls. You don't see the girls hanging around with the guys... The girls just react differently because they act all nervous around the guys saying 'oh this guy might like me' or 'I'm starting to like him'. Guys seem to be a bit shy too and say I better keep quiet or else 'she might start liking me or I might like her'. They mightn't want to say anything in case they'd make a fool of themselves, but it's different in Australia you could say anything to a girl and she'd either laugh or not and that would be it. (Eoin, 13)

The nervousness he observed among girls in Ireland was, Eoin thought, evident in their constant pursuit of physical enhancement and validation.

> One thing I've noticed over here is the amount of girls that wear makeup, they just pack it on and they wear fake tan. I looked and said 'are you serious they all wear makeup?' In Australia they might wear a bit of makeup or none at all ... They wouldn't care what people think but here girls do care and guys do care about what people think.

An interviewee from Russia said it had been much easier for her to be friends with boys there than it was in Ireland.

> Before I started travelling with my parents and came here about four years ago I had a lot of boys who were friends. I had only two best friends and they were boys. Now it's different. Maybe it's because I've grown up or maybe it's because people think it's not realistic to be friends with boys here. (Rebecca, 16)

In adolescence boys and girls test relationships and boundaries with one another and their nervousness might simply be due to their natural growing interest in sexual acceptability. But since adolescents in other countries are likely to experience the same interests, this alone cannot account for why inter-sex friendships are considered unrealistic among Irish adolescents. Over two thirds of the respondents spoke of being shy or nervous around the opposite sex and differentiated their experiences from the interactions they had witnessed between boys and girls in other countries or had seen on TV.

Maintaining a physical impression

Not only was embodied capital in aesthetic and athletic form advantageous for the validation of membership of prestigious teams and for maintaining them, but it was also vital for inter-sex encounters, where adolescents were intent on making a physical impression. However, just as lapses in physical display were sufficient for them to be dismissed from a team, they could also be the death of romantic relationships. The type of unstable relationships talked about by Giddens (1991), Sennet (1994) and Turner, B (1999) are apparent here in an entirely bodily dimension. Giddens observes how relationships may break down if the self-commitments of one party outweigh their commitment to the relationship. For the youths in this study, relationships seemed to break down because they lacked individualised commitment to the self, particularly to the aesthetic-athletic dimension of the self.

Many of the participants described how they would not date or form romantic relationships with people they did not find attractive. Physical attractiveness was emphasised over and above qualities such as friendship and companionship.

> Boys want girls to have a good-looking face and wouldn't want them to be fat or anything. They don't really care what they're like, they only really care what they look like. They don't really care if it's someone to talk to. Most of the time it's just about how they look. (Josh, 13)

> All my friends are always going on about fellas who are gorgeous and no mention if he's sound. They like muscles and a boy band pretty look. (Tara, 15)

This toned pretty look evoked acceptance. It was placed in opposition to the overweight body: many of the adolescents asserted that they would not enter a relationship with someone they considered to be overweight and would terminate a relationship if their partner gained too much weight.

> You don't want to be going with someone who's not good-looking ... If she changed and I was good friends with her, I'd say I'd keep going out with her but if she changed to completely obese, I don't think so [laughs]. (Mark, 12)

> You wouldn't want to be going out with one that was stupid or acted stupid or even looked stupid. If she was fat you wouldn't want to go out with her. I'd tell her to loose the weight. Tell her she's put on a load of weight and she should loose it because she looked better when she wasn't fat ... I might stay with her if she was sound but if she got real, real fat then no [laughs]. (Kevin, 13)

> When you're with your friends you wouldn't want to be seen with your girlfriend if she's obese. The first thing any guy would do, if I'm being honest here, I'd probably dump her, just because you wouldn't want to bump into your friends and they'd be like 'Is that your girlfriend?' (Eoin, 13)

> Honestly I wouldn't go out with them if they were ugly. For me personality is very important as well so I wouldn't judge them solely on looks. Like I'm not that shallow but in my book they couldn't be very overweight. It's just the way I've been brought up to think about that sort of person. (Brian, 16)

Although Brian was aware that it is unacceptable to judge someone exclusively on the basis of looks and tried not to do so, he believed he had been socially schooled that it was normal to judge people by their bodies. Youths associated being overweight with a lack of care and control over the body and therefore a reason for terminating a relationship.

> You can't be going out with a dog or whatever. You have to find her attractive. She has to look good and I just don't find overweight girls attractive. Like I

know there's personality and everyone's sorta bullshitting on about it. If she is boring as anything you're just going to have to tell her to take a hike. Also you wouldn't want her to let herself go. If she did, I don't know [long pause]. I don't know. It's a hard one but I probably would dump her yeah. Yeah, I would. (Enda, 16)

I couldn't go with someone who was really fat or someone who just let themselves go. (Gillian, 16)

I couldn't go with a guy who just didn't care and ate loads. I just think that's totally unattractive ... If your fella put on weight you'd just want him to be the way he was before he put it on and I wouldn't be able to get the picture of what he was like before out of my head. (Lynn, 16)

In short, those deemed to possess socially validated bodies were socially enabled because they had a greater chance of accessing and maintaining relationships. And their acceptance into a relationship further confirmed the validated status of their body.

Social and physical validation was enhanced when their partner in the relationship was also rated as physically attractive. They came to be seen as an ideal couple and the validation of both parties was perpetuated so long as physical attractiveness was maintained.

It generally says that you're good-looking to have a good-looking partner. It is a statement. If you have a really good-looking couple they compliment each other, like Posh and Becks, they seem to fit together as a classic example of what you want in a couple. (Brian, 16)

Thus popularity and prestige were increased on the basis of being part of an ideal couple.

It means that they are more important than other people. Gives them better self-esteem. They feel better because they have a better boyfriend and they have a higher ego knowing that they can do better. (Amy, 13)

For a guy, all his friends think he's great, as he's with a good-looking girl. This means that he'd be more popular and other people would want to be him. (Shannon, 14)

If she's gorgeous other people will fancy her as well and you could say 'oh I got her first'. (Mark, 12)

Within the ideal couple, status is created through the combined embodied capital of both partners, with one offering validation to the other through their continued acceptance within the relationship.

Conclusion

Acceptance among peers is a multifaceted process and adolescents struggle for a form of recognition that will validate their social standing among their peers. This chapter has illustrated the importance of body validation for the attainment and maintenance of social status within school and peer contexts. It reveals taken for granted intricacies that demand complex negotiation among young girls and even more among boys in their pursuit of peer acceptance.

The teenage boys I spoke with were keen to distance themselves from over association with academic pursuits. Although they acknowledged that this type of 'institutional' or educational capital (Bourdeiu, 1984) was important, they saw a need to neutralise engagement in academic activities with involvement in extra-curricular and especially sporting activities. These boys indicated that involvement in common interests such as sport was vital for establishing friendships and for enabling longevity. Sport provided a common geographical and conversational space for these boys to gain acceptance. But while acceptance may be based on an interest and involvement in sport; prestige and popularity depend on recognition within specific team sports. Displays of physical athleticism were essential for reception onto such acclaimed teams and being on one perpetuated their physical athleticism. The data suggested that a constant push for athletic perfection was necessary to retain a place on such teams. Thus the sports field becomes a site of physical warfare, where battles are played out not only among opposition teams but also against fellow team members in the competition to retain team positions and the social status this affords. Some youths referred to the social status that famous sports stars had achieved on the basis of their athleticism and they synthesised athleticism with aestheticism.

The narratives in this chapter reveal the significance of the aesthetic-athletic body in accessing romantic relationships. The young people represented the 'hetero-normativity' (Mac an Ghaill, 1994) of romantic relationships while emphasising the role of the body in constructing and securing such relationships. Chapter One pointed to the validation of a certain body forms such as the aesthetic-athletic body because of its enabling qualities and this chapter examined how this body form is enabling in accessing and stabilising peer relations. But are some body forms viewed as disabling in the pursuit of social validation? This question is explored in Chapter Four.

4

Rejected Bodies

Introduction

Adolescence is a time when being accepted among peers is immensely affirming but when their rejection is profoundly disturbing. Peer rejection takes the form of labelling, slagging, teasing, taunting, back-stabbing, abusing and outright excluding. It is often focused on identifying perceived inadequacies in other youths and categorising them on that basis. According to those who took part in this study, categorisation on the basis of perceived inadequacies is normalised within adolescent peer relations. Because one's body rather than one's personality is constantly on display to others, it becomes an obvious target for identifying inadequacies.

Categorising individuals because they are embodied in a particular way can be enabling, as in the case of the aesthetic-athletic body. This chapter examines how youths who fall too far either side of the ideal image come to be haunted by their deviation from it. They fail to attain the body validation which enables access to particular peer networks. The narratives indicate how those who are deemed to be too underweight or too overweight are categorised as lacking the embodied capital necessary for validation and are frequently stigmatised within their school and peer communities. A strategic allocation of power appears to lie at the heart of this stigmatisation: teens attempt to promote their own social image through the demotion of others'. The chapter ends with a consideration of the emotional impact of being stigmatisated and the strategies for trying to cope with it.

How stigmatising is normalised

According to Goffman (1963b), our everyday interactions inevitably present to us people who possess attributes which we regard as undesirable, even bad, dangerous or weak. Goffman holds that we make downward estimations of such individuals and they are 'thus reduced in our minds from a whole and usual person to a tainted, discounted one' and asserts that some people may be stigmatised because of a perceived 'discrepancy between the virtual and actual social identity' (1963b:12-13). Stigmatisation may result from what is deemed to be an 'abnormal' social practice, personal characteristic or abomination of the body. Any of the above can be sufficient for individuals to be stigmatised by those who are viewed as 'normal' (Goffman, 1963b). I found that the teenagers tended to categorise their peers within groupings similar to 'normal' and 'stigmatised'; I also found an overarching sense of stigmatisation as normal. It seemed they could be stigmatised because of any perceived inadequacy in their personal or physical identity. All had been well schooled on the vastness of stigmatisation. The cause could be anything from revealing where they lived, to letting their hair grow a centimetre too long.

> My friends call me 'the bogger'. I don't have a bogger accent but they're like 'Oh my God, did you hear the way she said that word? They call you a bogger if you're from Derryvale but Derryvale is not a bogger place. They all think I'm a bogger. I'm the bogger of the year. (Sarah, 16)

> I live in Killtown, so I'm not from Dublin. I get slagged for being a farmer because I'm from Wicklow. I don't even have a farm. (Cian, 16)

It is interesting that even though neither Sarah nor Cian saw themselves fitting the labels they had been assigned, they informed me of these stigmatised aspects of their identities without being asked. These labels, albeit undesirable aspects of their identities appear to have been internalised to become a part of how they describe themselves socially.

The vast majority of stigmas discussed related to 'blemishes' or 'abnormalities' of the body or its presentation.

> There was a boy in my class and because his clothes were all cheap stuff from like … non brand names, he used to get slagged for that because he wore the same kind of runners all the time. People would call him 'cheapo' because they would wear the newest gear and the newest runners. (Ger, 13)

> I wear a lot of make-up and black clothes. We're called Goths because of this and because we like rock music and we kind of get the piss kicked out of us. Like two weeks ago I was walking down the road with my friend and I had my hair kind of waxed into little pink dreadlocks, I was wearing white make-up and black eye liner. This gang of townie scumbag bitches walked past and ...they started screaming at us, calling us ugly for no reason. (Tara, 15)

Tara and her friends faced stigmatisation most places they went. Another participant, Rebecca labelled herself 'weird' because others told her she was because she spoke with an American accent. Daniel was labelled 'scruffy' because he failed to get his hair cut. Darren had long hair too, and was called 'girlie'. Lynn was known as 'redzer' because of her red hair. If, as Goffman suggests (1963b), a stigmatised group consists of people with some form of abnormality or weakness, every participant in the study was at some point considered abnormal or weak . Everyone had memories of being stigmatised for one reason or another, with most relating this to a perceived deviation from the socially validated body.

The adolescents felt that enduring labels and insults was an inevitable part of survival in their school and social communities. Some equated stigmatisation with bullying and said how prevalent it was.

> Bullying is a big problem. Some are bullied because they are different or they look different or because they like different types of music or because they believe in different things like religion. People don't respect you if you're not in the majority. (Darren, 12)

> It [bullying] happens all the time because boys are always slagging each other to their faces and trying to annoy each other. Most of the time it's only messing but sometimes it is serious, and they get annoyed about it, it might have gone too far. (Josh, 13)

> Lots of people worry about being bullied. At break you might get knocked down and then everyone would gather round you and laugh for like a minute. Everyone's going to get laughed at at some stage. You'd be always aware of it. (Evan, 13)

This normalisation of stigmatisation produced a population of youths who were constantly self-checking and self-conscious of any aspect of their identity that might be stigmatised. Boys mostly stigmatised through verbal or physical abuse.

> Say a fella brought a girl down and she was horrible, we [girls] wouldn't say anything but the fellas would be slagging him and putting her down even if she's standing there, they'd put her down ... if there's anything wrong with her. Like if she's a bit big or if she has a turn in her eye. They put me down about my hair, they say 'look at the fringe' and they slag me. I do take it as a mess but sometimes you feel as if they are being serious with you and you say 'God I'm going' and you just walk off. You'd feel very low. (Anna, 16)

Girls, on the other hand, were aware of other girls labelling them behind their backs.

> My friends are always bitching about people so I worry what they might say about me behind my back too. It could be really mean and hurtful but I wouldn't know. (Sarah, 16)

Whatever the method of stigmatisation, the process itself was normalised and its harmful effects generally deliberate. Goffman neglects the intentional nature of stigmatisation, claiming that 'normals mean no harm; when they do, it is because they don't know better' (1963b:141). It seems impossible to escape stigma in some form, so even those who stigmatise must be aware of its harmful impact. Thus stigmatisation has an intentional dimension and this may explain why the body is a prime target. Youths' bodies, unlike their personalities, are continuously on public display. There is little people can do to conceal the body, aside from clothing it, so the body will be targeted to cause maximum pain and powerlessness.

Stigmatising the thin body

The teenagers told me how those who were seen as too thin or too fat seldom attained body validation from their peers, and were accordingly stigmatised. Being too thin or too fat was a major issue in their choice of which body image silhouettes they would most and least like to have. Twenty-six of the thirty youths picked the overweight body as the one they would least like to have, and four the underweight body. This fits with how teenage boys tended to assign a status of body validation to those who could prove their physical strength (see Chapter Two) and how the most prestigious social positions in their schools were reserved for those who were best at physical team sports (see Chapter Three). Since the strong, controlled and athletic body is particularly enabling, so it is little wonder that some boys identified extreme thinness as being socially disabling.

The boys described how thin boys were stigmatised through overt name-calling. They were schooled in a way that permitted little discussion around the physical qualities they admired in other boys, lest they be labelled 'girlie' or 'gay'. However, they were also schooled in a way that permitted overt labelling of those who exhibited undesirable physical qualities. This intentional identification of flaws has significant influence on the allocation of power. When one person directs attention at the flaws of another, he may be trying to detract attention from his own or make himself appear worthier of body validation. Goffman proposes that stigmatised individuals should ignore any comment directed at them or try to re-educate those making it.

> Either no notice should be taken or the stigmatised individual should make an effort at sympathetic re-education of the normals, showing him, point for point, quietly and with delicacy, that in spite of appearance the stigmatised individual is, underneath it all, a fully-human being. (Goffman, 1963b:141)

However, perhaps it is more difficult to educate those who stigmatise on the nature of another's stigma, if it is their desire to keep the stigmatised individual excluded and subordinate.

The stigmatisation of thin boys was characterised by both verbal and physical domination. Many of the participants relayed stories about themselves or their peers being targeted because they were thin. There was a definite sense of verbal and physical subordination that left youths feeling vulnerable and threatened.

> I know three guys like this who can't put on weight. One guy can actually suck in his stomach so much that you can see his lungs ... One guy is eight and a half stone and about six foot tall. I can pick him up and put him over my shoulder and he can't do anything about it. It does get them down. They feel threatened by the fact that people feel they can knock them down just because they're so light and they see that as a problem. They'd prefer to look more masculine and have a bulky look to them. One guy always talks about how frail he feels because of how thin he is. He has a good personality and gets along with people, but, at the same time, he's broken his sternum three times just from people messing around with him. (Cathal, 16)

> One guy isn't terribly small but he's really, really skinny and I'd say he weighs about eight stone. He does be thrown around the class ... He loves wrestling too and playing around but he's usually the dummy because he's so skinny and they just lift him up and throw him around. (Andy, 16)

Both boys used the phrase 'messing around' to indicate playful camaraderie. Nevertheless, their bodies were used to make them feel subordinate and lacking in masculine strength; the very quality that was a prerequisite for validation of the male body. One boy identified himself as the one who was thrown around in his class.

> In class I just get thrown around the place. I'm only nine stone, eleven pounds so I'm like way too light and I get thrown around the place. If there's any messing in the class I'm the first one to get thrown out of the place. (Enda, 16)

The stigmatising stories told by Cathal, Andy and Enda all reveal a sense of intent. Adolescent boys are never thrown around a room accidentally. Although Enda stated that he was not particularly bothered by this domination he also admitted that physical activities made him feel powerless and lacking in control.

> In sport I prefer to do things where I can control whether I'm going to get hurt or not, if I'm climbing a mountain or something like that. I have no problems going off a twenty foot cliff but if I'm going up against a big guy on a team I'd be cacking myself because you don't know what he's going to do, whereas if I'm going off the edge of a cliff I know that I'm in control, if I fall it's my fault like. I don't find things like that scary but I don't like when someone has control over my fate I suppose. (Enda, 16)

It is possible that Enda's fear of contact sports is a manifestation of his feeling of powerlessness due to being physically dominated in the classroom. The boys attended different schools, which indicates that stigmatisation is normalised.

Stigmatisation of the thin body has emotional consequences that highlight the immense importance of attaining body validation. Eve drew a parallel between stigmatisation and bullying, and related how it had almost fatal consequences for her brother.

> He [brother] doesn't like the way he looks because he's small. Well all my brothers are small but he doesn't have any muscles or anything. He wants to be bigger so that's why he's joining the gym. When he was in third year he was getting bullied. One night he locked himself in the toilet and went to kill himself. I was sobbing. I know I'm always saying I hate him, but I do love him … He was slitting his wrists and that night my mam had to bring him to the hospital. He still has the scars there today. It's horrible. (Eve, 13)

How worrying that this young boy had been so severely stigmatised for being thin that he attempted to end his life. The bullying had left physical and emotional scars on not only her brother but also on this thirteen year old girl and her whole family.

Girls gave no accounts of being physically or verbally abused for being too thin, although two girls suggested that boys might call very slender girls 'anorexic' or 'matchsticks'. Out of a total of the 123 girls sampled in the study through open-ended question and answer sheets, only one stated that she wanted to participate because she felt she was stigmatised for being too thin.

> If you were with a group of friends they'd be saying 'oh my God you can see her ribs' or 'you can see her collar bones' or something and they'd talk underneath their breath and then you get really self-conscious and you're like 'oh my God, can you?' and then you'd get all paranoid and it's just like a snowball, it just keeps going. (Sarah, 16)

Sarah spoke of being categorised by girls through hushed tones and surveillance. It was the boys who overtly called them names.

Being stigmatised for being thin made boys feel particularly vulnerable and uncertain, although both boys and girls who discussed the problems of being thin admitted that they would rather be underweight than overweight, explaining that overweight teens were often perceived as 'abnormal' or 'unnatural'.

> If you ask anyone like 'would you prefer to be anorexic or would you prefer to be obese?' They'd all say anorexic. (Sarah, 16)

Passing the body as 'normal'

When explaining why overweight children are most stigmatised the teenagers highlighted the visual nature of the body. Goffman also emphasises the visible nature of bodily stigmas, unlike stigmas relating to an individual's personality, practices or past experiences.

> Visibility, of course, is a crucial factor. That which can be told about an individual's social identity at all times during his daily round and by all persons he encounters therein will be of great importance to him. (Goffman, 1963b:65)

The adolescents confirmed the overall importance of visibility in the stigmatising processes, but they distinguished between the visibility of the thin body and that of the fat body. The visual nature of the thin body made it easier for those considered too underweight for body validation to conceal it. With the right clothes they could 'get away with it' whereas clothes could not conceal the overweight teens' deviation from what the participants designated as the 'natural', 'normal' body.

> I think being really fat is worse … because if you're really skinny you can kind of wear clothes that make you look at bit chunkier and you can get away with it but if you're fat it's harder to get away with it. (Rob, 16)

> You can hide that you're too skinny but not really when you're overweight. (Amy, 13)

Recent studies stress the prevalence of obesity among Irish children and teenagers. Over 300,000 children in Ireland were estimated in 2005 to be overweight or obese, a figure projected to rise annually by 10,000 (*The Report of the National Taskforce on Obesity*, 2005:3). Yet the teens I talked to thought that overweight kids in school stood out.

> Real big is the worst. If he's just real fat; he'd stand out in a crowd. If you saw him you'd notice him because he's just so fat … He wouldn't be fit at all. (Kevin, 13)

They held that it was 'normal' or 'natural' to be thin at their age and that overweight youths were categorised and even castigated because they deviated from this norm.

> Mostly the people in school would be thin so they'd be the bigger group and might slag all the fat people. (Barry, 16)

> I'd say both fat people and small and skinny people would get slagged because people would slag them because of their shape. But I'd say the fat would get more probably because it's more natural to be thin at our age. (Josh, 13)

> If they're absolutely scrawny but had a nice face you'd still go with them. If they were absolutely obese but had a nice face, I don't think so because it's not natural. (Barry, 16)

Some believed it was natural for someone to be underweight but not overweight.

> Nobody is naturally fat but some people are naturally thin and they just can't put on weight. (Tara, 15)

Overweight teens were often blamed for their weight because it was seen as being of their own doing.

The meaning of 'fat'

The adolescents largely confirmed negative attitudes towards the fat body reflecting thinking that is 'fatphobic or sizist comprising prejudice and discrimination towards people who are seen as fat in everyday life' (Monaghan, 2007:68). Attitudes towards bodies that are perceived to have something wrong with them can range from 'disgust and abhorrence to heartfelt pity', according to Carol Thomas (2003:64). Many youths responded to the fat body with disgust rather than pity because they viewed fat as unnatural and something that should not be flaunted or exposed. Over half the adolescents who spoke with me expressed their revulsion at 'seeing flab'. They strongly rejected the exposure of fat flesh.

> Like my friend is big but it's just that she wears low bottoms and high tops and she has a stomach that would kind of flab over. And you'd love to kind of say to her 'wear your top down a bit' because it's not nice I don't think. (Lynn, 16)

> It's okay for women as well as long as they keep it all hidden away rather than wearing belly tops. (Cian, 16)

> It's the fashion to have things down on your hips. There are a few big girls I know and they wear their trousers down on their hips and their bellies would be hanging out. It's not a pretty sight. (Caoimhe, 16)

> It's the stomach – if it's rippled, it's horrible, yuck. (Brian, 16)

> I have a problem with people going around flaunting fat. A lot of people seem to let the fat hang out and they don't seem to care, both males and females. I remember seeing a guy a few months ago who was wearing a t-shirt and his gut actually hung out under the t-shirt. I remember thinking that was pretty disgusting. I've seen both do it and it's not particularly enjoyable to look at. (Cathal, 16)

Boys and girls alike voiced their concerns about keeping fat concealed. This, along with their alignment of the thin body with the 'natural' and the overweight body with the 'unnatural', is a product of general attitudes towards fat in the western world.

Theorists who have contributed to the sociology of the body have explained the socially symbolic meaning attached to being fat in western cultures. Gordon (1990), Featherstone (1991), Frank (1991), Turner, B, (1984, 1992, 1996), Baudrillard (1998), Grogan (1999), Redmond (2003), Gill, Henwood and McLean (2005), Monaghan (2005) and many others agree that within an aesthetically driven world, the fat body is perceived as 'indicative of laziness, lack of discipline, unwillingness to conform' (Bordo, 1993:195). Terms such as 'laziness', 'lack of discipline' or 'unwillingness', relate as much to the mindset of an individual as to their body. Goffman suggests that this is a case of others imputing 'a wide range of imperfections on the basis of the original one' (1963b:15-16). Judgements do not stop at the immediate physical presentation of the individual. Rather, they impute 'certain characteristics and personality features on the basis of initial presentation', which means that 'the discrediting of the person is not limited to the superficial but takes in the whole identity (Frost, 2005:80). The mindset of the individual is judged on the basis of the overweight body, just as it is blamed for the overweight body.

> You think they're lazy, that they eat a lot of fast food. Okay it could be hormonal but I don't think a lot of people actually think that when they see someone heavy walking down the street. (Gillian, 16)

Other participants confirmed Gillian's suspicions that most attribute fat not to physical but to personal failure. This resonates with Gill, Henwood and McLean's findings that being fat is not only about looking unattractive – it is also about being viewed as a moral failure (2005:55).

> If you see someone like that you can just sort of tell what sort of person they are. They're lazy sometimes. They're just fat. If you see someone's flab you always just say he doesn't really care about his appearance at all. He doesn't really give it much thought. He just goes around eats and then turns out like that. (Evan, 13)

Fatphobia and sizism could also take the form of infantilising (Monaghan, 2007:81): one boy referred to in this study was labelled 'stupid' because he was overweight.

> A boy in my class was quite big and he used to get slagged by the people in the older class ... If they were playing football and your man fell, they'd start calling him fat and stuff and they'd say 'oh look at you, you're so stupid'... There was a girl in my class that people used to slag as well because she was

big. Just the same stuff, if she did something stupid they'd start slagging her about being fat. She was just slagged because she was fat even though they mightn't use the word fat, it was always because she was fat. (Ger, 13)

This boy was labelled stupid because he was fat and was said to be fat because he was stupid. Comments directed at both mind and body illustrate the embodied nature of stigmatisation, whereby the psychological and the physiological are simultaneously targeted.

Fat: a four letter word?

The adolescents wholly accepted that fat people are generally described in critical and derogatory terms and that their differential treatment was entirely normalised. The teenagers were aware that judging people on the basis of their body shape appeared shallow, yet felt that they had been socially schooled to judge people in this way.

> You can see it happening everywhere and people being slagged about their weight all the time ... Fat people are treated very differently. Just the general image in itself. They say never judge a book by its cover but that's not what teenagers do, teenagers do judge books by their covers. I don't want to fall into that category but I do. It's the way I've been brought up and I've been taught to think about how you should classify a person or give them labels and that's what I find myself doing. (Brian, 16)

All the adolescents recalled instances where they or their peers had been stigmatised because of their weight. Their stories revealed how both boys and girls were verbally and physically abused because they had somehow failed to situate their bodies within a narrow realm of validity and conformity.

> I wouldn't say they're [overweight youths] treated very nicely. There's one guy who's in my year and everyone just calls him a beached whale, stupid stuff. (Barry, 16)

> They'd just get slagged going along and would be looked down on I suppose. Wouldn't be treated on the same level as other people. There's one guy in third year and he's called 'slim shady' because he's so huge. (Andy, 16)

> Even if people don't know them they say 'look at her, she's so fat'. Some people that are overweight get a lot of abuse and a lot of name-calling. (Caoimhe, 16)

> This guy who was in my class last year, they'd say 'giggly arse' and 'giggly bum' to him and then they'd kick him. They used to call him 'watermelon with legs' and 'fatty' and all this. It's normal for things like that. (Evan, 13)

> Obviously the slags you get are really bad ... Every time I walked by they'd turn around and start screaming 'you fat bitch' at me. (Tara, 15)

Gordon suggests that by the time children reach elementary school, they have already absorbed widely disseminated convictions that associate fat with negative personal characteristics (1990:85). Similarly, Conner and Armitage found that children are schooled on the stigmatisation of overweight peers very early on.

> [This prejudice] begins in childhood, with children preferring not to play with overweight peers and assigning negative adjectives to drawings of overweight individuals. In adulthood, overweight individuals tend to be rated as less active and athletic, but also less intelligent, hardworking, successful and popular ... Such negative views of the overweight individual appear to be particularly common in individualistic cultures where individuals are held responsible for their own fate. (Connor and Armitage, 2000:77-78)

Lynch and Lodge also found that small and thin, and especially overweight boys were teased and bullied in school, and a superior masculine status given to those with strong and powerful bodies (1999). You might imagine that a heavy lad would be strong enough to protect himself from physical abuse in a way that the skinny youths could not. But this is not about the domination of the strong and the subordination of the weak *per se*. It is about a complex and strategic allocation of power through the domination of those who feel they are worthy of body validation and the subordination of those whom they feel are not.

The teenagers were in no doubt as to how the term 'fat' should be received, thanks to the intentional and confrontational abuse they witnessed around them. According to Monaghan:

> Fat is not a four-letter word, but it is often intended, and received, as a term of abuse. This is compounded by what I call *bodyism* – the cultural belief that the whole body, perhaps more so than the face (Synnott, 1989), reflects individual character. The 'f' word is therefore less than ideal. (2005:83)

Even when labelling a person 'fat' is not intended as a form of abuse, the categorisation can be interpreted as in itself offensive and wounding. The adolescents described the harrowing effect such labelling had on their peers.

> With my friend no matter where she goes there's always someone calling her 'fat bitch' and 'big belly'... The boys would just say it to her you know if they were playing football and they would say 'oh go on, you can't run for the football, you're too fat'. I do pity her. I know she just sits on the stairs at night. (Eve, 13)

> You'd just be playing football or something and someone would just say something that would really hurt her feelings and she'd get really upset. They'd say 'look at the state of you' and 'you look disgusting' and more to her. She is a bit overweight but not really. She'd get really upset about it because she's conscious of her weight anyway and then when people say things like that to her it doesn't make her feel great. (Amy, 13)

Overweight teens were often excluded from activities that demanded pace and athleticism, the very activities that are so significant in the assignment of social and physical validation (see Chapter Three).

While Goffman makes little reference to the emotional impact of stigmatisation, he does acknowledge that it makes those who are stigmatised self-conscious. He observes that the standards the stigmatised individual has 'incorporated from the wider society equip him to be intimately alive to what others see as his failings' (1963b:17-18). As well as heightened self-consciousness, the youths' narratives described how overweight adolescents were continuously reminded of their failings. While many of us can become oblivious to our specific embodiment within the humdrum of daily life, the latent or '*disappearing*' body is much less likely among stigmatised individuals (Leder, 1990). Moreover:

> If the properly functioning body recedes from our consciousness, however, Leder also recognizes that pain, illness or the embarrassment caused by 'slips' or 'gaffes' (Goffman, 1956) can make the body reappear with a vengeance. (Shilling, 2003:184)

For the youths I spoke to, being categorised as fat embarrassed them and thus heightened their bodily consciousness.

Interestingly, when girls were overtly teased about their weight, it was by boys. In employing these labelling practices, the boys assert male power over girls, who are 'ridiculed, put down, humiliated and objectified' (Dalley-Trim, 2007:202). For the girls I spoke to, being labelled fat created a level of bodily consciousness that precipitated what could be viewed as body dismorphia. Some participants told me they were labelled as fat, even though I could see no justification. We need to differentiate between being fat and 'feeling' fat: being called fat led to feeling fat and they lived with the emotional consequences of this feeling.

> All my brothers tell me I'm fat. One goes on about it for ages, even you know when I'm down at the flats and I'm playing with my friend, he'd say 'oh that's the first time I've ever seen you running'. Like they can really hurt you the way they keep on saying it to you ... Just after playing a game, I'd sit up for a rest and it'd all come back to me again and I just shake my head. (Eve, 13)

> I have often been upset because sometimes they call me things and say stuff about my weight, but most of the girls they don't really get jeered at because most of them are pretty. The rest of them would just get one or two comments and then they'd be let alone. They continuously have a go at me though, like every Friday. (Molly, 13)

All Molly's friends were labelled in some way, which confirms that stigmatisation was normalised. Molly found the labelling directed at her weight relentless. She internalised these labels and set herself apart from her 'pretty' friends, in a category more in keeping with the negative labels attributed to her. Some of the participants conveyed a strong sense of what Goffman hypothesises: that a person's awareness of their deviation from what is expected can lead to 'self-hate and self-derogation ... when only he and a mirror are about' (Goffman, 1963b:18).

The adolescents were acutely aware of the emotional impact of stigmatisation on overweight teens. Many talked about a fear of becoming fat because of the feelings of self-consciousness, self-hatred and social rejection they expected this would bring.

> You feel low if you're after putting on weight, you can see yourself that you're after putting on weight. And you'd feel real low in yourself and you'd feel as if no one wants to be with you. (Anna, 15)

They constantly related being fat to restricted social participation and inclusion. However, they also highlighted the strategies teenagers used to cope with the restrictions that their communities had placed on them.

Coping with stigmatisation

Goffman proposes that one way of coping with stigmatisation is to reduce the possibility of its occurrence through avoidance strategies. He suggests that "mixed contacts' – the moments when stigmatised and normal are in the same 'social situation" (Goffman, 1963b:23) – can cause much tension for those on both sides. Therefore, 'the very anticipation of such contacts can of course lead normals and the stigmatised to arrange life so as to avoid them' (*ibid*). One third of the interviewees said that overweight adolescents try to remove themselves from the possibility of stigmatisation in this way. But teenagers cannot totally rearrange their day to avoid stigmatisation as their days are not their own to rearrange. They are obliged to attend school and therefore face the frequent normality of rejection. It seemed that when they do have authority over how to spend their time they spend it alone. Away from labelling and sneering, the world can seem less harsh. None of the teenagers I spoke to considered themselves so fat that they would prefer to spend time alone than with their friends but many said that if they became overweight they would not want to socialise or go out in public.

The teenagers identified the main reasons for overweight people choosing to be alone as lack of confidence, shyness, a fear of judgement and the unlikelihood of making friends .

> They don't have the confidence if they're really fat, they don't usually go out much. At my age when they're fat they don't think they'll make friends at all and they just stay in their house. (Evan, 13)

> They're really shy and they're just afraid to get out there because of the way they look. (Rob, 16)

> I'd say if you were really fat you wouldn't be as prepared to be out and about and for people to see you. You'd hide away more. People do that. If you were just really thin it wouldn't be as bad so you wouldn't mind being seen. (Cian, 16)

Self-enclosure was not always viewed as an act of free will and some interviewees acknowledged that constant stigmatisation pushed youths into isolation as a form of self-protection.

> Everyone in the area keeps slagging her and she wouldn't come down for ages because people were calling her fat. (Eve, 13).

> There is a big fella and they do slag him all the time but he's after loosing loads of weight ... He doesn't really come down anymore. He used to always be down. (Mary, 13)

Overweight youths were constantly battling to cope with insults and stares. They were forced to adopt defence strategies against stigmatisation in class, in the playground, in their local community. Self-enclosure allowed them to draw breath, away from the persistent and consistent labelling.

The adolescents felt that overweight people are often embarrassed because of their weight and one adolescent spoke about the embarrassment being associated with an overweight person would cause.

> If they're very overweight they just wouldn't fit in. You wouldn't want to be seen with them because you'd be embarrassed because everyone would be looking at him and then staring at you and saying 'what are you doing with him?' (Kevin, 13)

This may be one reason why overweight adolescents turned towards each other for friendship. Stigmatised individuals may feel less tense around people with like stigmas (Goffman, 1963b). For overweight adolescents, this is escapism similar to self-enclosure, giving them a break from abusive labels when around people of the same size. Self-grouping by size and weight was certainly alive and well in the schools I visited.

> They may just sit down by themselves or with a few other people the same. (Eoin, 13)

> If you see one big person, you'll probably see three. They'll all hang round together. (Caoimhe, 16)

> There's a group of them that are friends and they're all big ... The three of them are very, very big. If you had to pick out big people you'd pick the three of them. Maybe it is just coincidental that the three of them are friends or maybe they are on the same wave length. It could be a possibility that they feel rejected by other groups. But it's not just them, there's loads more groups. Like there's two big people in sixth year that always hang around together and even more in the junior years. (Andy, 16)

Segregation on the basis of body size was certainly normalised. Mixed size grouping increased the risk of stigmatisation and levels of self-consciousness.

> Fat people are put into a different group. People who are fat or chubby tend to stick to that group and thin people stick with thin people. That's what my cousin does because she's fat. She tends to stick with people who are the

same size as her instead of going with skinny people because she thinks they are talking about her behind her back. She cares what they think about her all the time. (Chloe, 13)

I'd be conscious that I might get overweight and I wouldn't feel very good about myself or like going out with people who would be a lot skinnier than me. (Amy, 13)

There seems to be a dual process at play in these segregation strategies. Overweight teens voluntarily form friendships with other overweight teens as a way of reducing stigmatisation, but they are also placed in these groups because of social rejection by other peers.

The teenagers described self-stigmatisation as a tactic used by overweight people to cope with stigmatisation. Self-stigmatisation has at its core a logic of 'if you can't beat 'em, join 'em'. Self-stigmatising youths are those who have the ability to laugh at their own weight and thus be categorised as a particular type of fat person.

There's two kinds of fat people. Some think no one's going to want to know them because they're fat and then others just try and then make friends. There's one lad who's very overweight but he says he doesn't care and he's one of the most popular people in our year. There's very few that still have the confidence that he has when you're overweight. He's very funny. (Evan, 13)

One third of the teenagers used the term 'funny fat people' or something similar and on each occasion this required youths to be amusing about their own weight. Being able to laugh off labels or comments reduced the possibility of being stigmatised.

Like one of my friend's names is 'fat boy' and he thinks it's hilarious. He's not that fat but he thinks it's hilarious and he constantly makes comments about how fat he is … He'll refer to himself as festively plump. (Cathal, 16)

If you're a bit fat who cares, if you're a good laugh. Like if you can laugh about it too. If you're really fat and you're having a fight you can be just slagged because of your weight and a whole load of people think that funny. (Mark, 12)

There's no use slagging someone if they just laugh it off and agree. (Ger, 13)

Even if these youths do not really find stigmatisation funny, their funny *façade* allows them to negotiate access to groups that might otherwise reject them. Their humourous personalities compensate for any perceived physical inadequacies. Swain, too, found that compensating was a strategy used to cope with social exclusion.

> The major material bodily difference came from the impression of being over-weight, and my data is littered with disparaging references directed to boys and girls being 'a big fat blob', 'fat-boy', 'so fat', 'really fat', and so on. It was a serious handicap to boys' (or girls') attempts to establish peer group status, and boys needed to use other strategies and resources in order to compensate for it. (Swain, 2003:310)

The fact that compensating for being fat through poking fun at fat actually reduced stigmatisation indicates its intentional nature. Where obvious signs of harm were not apparent stigmatisation was significantly reduced. Overweight adolescents were less stigmatised in the long run if they participated in the seemingly hilarious practice of their own self-stigmatisation. However, as with self-enclosure and group segregation, self-stigmatisation does not appear to lead to body validation. It simply perpetuates prevailing perceptions of which body is validated and which body must compensate for its failure to be validated.

Conclusion

This chapter has described how adolescents are labelled and ridiculed because of their bodies. Goffman proposes a framework which looks at groups of 'normals' and 'stigmatised', but the teenagers' stories in this chapter have signalled the normalisation of stigmatisation. The narratives suggested that all children and adolescents are schooled on stigmatisation through experiencing it to some degree. However, for youths whose bodies fall too far either side of the validated body form, stigmatisation is more persistent and perhaps more aligned with bullying.

It was the overweight who were likely to face most ridicule and rejection. Teenagers emphasised the apparent intentional and confrontational nature of the stigmatising process aimed at the body. Taunting and abuse could be fully understood as being not so much the domination of physical strength over physical weakness but rather a mechanism for allocating power. It is, perhaps, an attempt by some to perpetuate their own perceived worthiness of physical validation by identifying and subordinating those who are unworthy.

The narratives in this chapter confirm Monaghan's assertion that though 'fat' may not be a four-letter word, it can be used and received as an abusive term (2005). Equally, Goffman's (1963b) idea that secondary labels are often applied to individuals on the basis of the first, was demonstrated by the labelling of overweight children as 'lazy', 'disgusting' and even 'stupid'. Labels relating to the body constantly schooled adolescents on the inescapability of their embodied state. Negative labels had a harsh emotional impact. Even when labels were unjustly assigned, they caused some participants to believe that their bodies deviated greatly from the bodies around them that were validated.

This chapter points to three strategies adopted by the teenagers deemed overweight to cope with stigmatisation. They chose self-confinement – a place safe from stigmatisation. And, whether through choice or lack of choice, overweight teens appeared to associate overwhelmingly with others of similar body size. The third strategy was self-stigmatisation – where overweight youths demonstrated an apparently unharmed demeanour towards negative labels by perpetuating their supposed hilarity. These strategies highlight the daily struggles faced by those who fail to attain body validation because they are perceived to be too fat. They indicate the battle of coping with rejection as well as the pursuit of acceptance. And they offer insight into why the teenagers so feared becoming fat. The next chapter gives an account of the problems faced by the teenagers in their efforts to avoid gaining weight.

5

Predictable Bodies

Introduction

Most children in the west experience a 'hypermarket of culture' which encourages them to 'accept everything, eat everything, touch everything' (Baudrillard, 1982:10). Teenagers are influenced by the press and advertising as to what images they should buy into (see Chapter One). The adolescents in this study stressed time and again that having a certain body form, such as an aesthetic-athletic type, enables access to friendship and romance, sport and activities. Those who are thinner and particularly fatter than this ideal body form are often stigmatised and rejected. However, these teenagers have been subject to years of food and drink advertising that is schooling them on the desirability of our vast choice of food. It has never been easier to become overweight, but it has never been harder to live with being so.

This chapter explores how teenagers synthesise the common marketing and availability of fast foods and junk foods with a western intolerance of the unregulated body. Theorists have long been writing about this intolerance and some discuss the desire to reach a point of body regulation that is beyond hunger (Turner. B., 1984, 1992, 1996; Bordo, 1993). The adolescents I spoke to viewed eating as enjoyable and sociable, but they were terrified of getting fat. These contradictory desires cause people of both sexes and all ages to feel guilty about eating. This chapter examines how adolescents employ regimes to ensure they maintain a validated body shape while at the same time indulging in the hypermarket of foods.

Tempting foods

The general expansion of the food market encourages adolescents to try more, enjoy more: live a little. Nowadays, people want to live and experience everything; 'looking, deciphering, studying doesn't move them' any longer (Baudrillard, 1982:10). Among the adolescents I spoke to, the localisation of global food choices and the cosmopolitan style of eating out, plus some financial independence, made lunching and dining with friends common practice. They saw eating as a source of sociality (Shilling, 2005:153). And they negotiated the cultural symbolism attached to particular foods. They strongly associated foods such as chocolate and sweets with happiness and comfort. Their feelings towards these foods largely reflected how they are marketed and the teenagers were acutely aware of this.

> It's [chocolate] everywhere, on the TV and advertisements and everywhere. Like the Cadbury's ads. It's like it will make us happy. Say if they're advertising bananas they wouldn't advertise the taste but with chocolate it's all about the taste and what's different about it than other bars. (Sandra, 13)

> Chocolate boosts your energy and all that and they have a nice taste off them ... They all have different tastes compared to say, a banana, like you eat that all the time but different chocolate bars taste different... We see everyone around us and all the ads. They always have ads like when your one was lying on the sofa and eating the dairy milk. She sinks down into the chair and they say she's making love to it. (Chloe, 13)

> I love sweets. I have a sweet tooth. We all have. Chocolate has a drug in it that makes us happy. (Mark, 12)

> I'd nearly have a bar or some sweets everyday... it's the sugar and because it tastes nice probably. It's like with chocolate it's not just plain chocolate that you get, there's lots of different bars with other things in them. It's just whatever's in them is really nice. (Josh, 13)

> Some ads make it look so relaxing because in the Galaxy ad it's raining out and she's just sitting there eating the Galaxy. Makes it look like you have to do that when it's raining out, just get a cup of tea and sit there. It's so relaxing because she's just sitting there with her Galaxy and the whole world is just walking by in the cold and it's lashing out. It's just so relaxing and when you're eating it you're not thinking about whether it's bad for you. (Caoimhe, 16)

It tastes nice and it's really calming. All the ads on the television make it seem so calming. In the Nestle Double Cream ad they have someone in brown clothes so it looks all soothing and everything ... It looks gorgeous and really tasty. You feel it would make you feel great. (Amy, 13)

Ahh chocolate ... All the ads make it look so gorgeous. Like the Galaxy ad where she closes the curtains and jumps onto the couch and the chocolate is sitting on the wrapper and she's about to eat it ... It seems like it will make you so happy. (Gillian, 16)

These young people were aware of the range of tempting foods that were available, thanks to their assiduous marketing.

They also talked about the popularity of fast food. This is hardly surprising given that fast food companies have spread out across the world, especially in the west. It seems that McDonalds' golden arches are globally more recognised than the Christian cross (Williams, 2005). One of fast food companies' striking features is the way they have targeted the younger population. In his book *Fast Food Nation* (2002), Schlosser suggests that food companies target children from an early age, schooling them in the attractiveness of their products. He observes that 'the aim of most children's advertising is straightforward: get kids to nag their parents and nag them well' (Schlosser, 2002:43). For parents who have little time to do domestic chores and who may feel guilty for not spending enough time with their children, junk food and fast food are treats to keep everyone happy. In Ireland, little has been spent on developing children's recreational facilities, leaving a gap that companies such as McDonalds and Burger King fill with adventurous play areas and novelty toys within a secure setting. Toy promotions may have little appeal for teenagers, but effectively socialise children early, encouraging a taste for their products and loyalty to the company and this carries into adolescence and beyond.

Fast food and junk food companies have penetrated school sports grounds through sponsorship of sporting initiatives for children. The Gaelic Athletic Association's 'Catch and Kick' programme promoting Gaelic football at primary school level was sponsored by McDonalds and so to was the association's 'Lift and Strike' programme for the promotion of hurling, which was also endorsed by pop singer Justin Timberlake. Sports equipment and clothing featuring McDonalds' distinctive golden arches was sent to children nationwide, no doubt intensifying their awareness of the company.

Fast food and junk food feature prominently in school canteens. Although Irish schools have not yet followed the United States in having companies such as McDonalds, Pizza Hut and Dominos supply food for cafeterias in public high schools, similar foods are provided in Irish secondary schools. The food on sale in the five schools I visited was depressingly similar. Children were invited to choose mainly from chips, burgers, hotdogs and sausage rolls. Muffins and doughnuts were also sold in the school canteens and chocolate bars, chewy bars, sweets, crisps and fizzy drinks in the school vending machines and tuck shops.

Despite the mandatory element of the school syllabus (Social, Personal and Health Education) that advises adolescents to eat healthy food, healthy food was generally unavailable in the schools these youths attended. This pattern is said to be changing, although where healthy foods are available they tend to be expensive. Banning unhealthy foods to promote healthy eating has been attempted, but chiefly in primary schools. Secondary schools which offer little alternative to junk foods and convenience foods leave the pupils with no other choices for lunch and contradicts the SPHE syllabus. The teenagers described the foods available in their schools – they were strikingly unvaried.

> If you go up to the shop, it's like all doughnuts and I'd say they sell hundreds of sausage rolls a day. It's lately that they started selling cream or jam or plain donuts. They sell all different kind of crisps and there's a drinks cabinet. You can order your roll at the 10 o'clock break and they have it ready for you at 12 o'clock. A lot of people would have [potato] wedges and breakfast roll. They have salad rolls as well but they wouldn't be as popular. (Andy, 16)

> You can get hotdogs, muffins, doughnuts, hamburgers, sausage rolls. (Evan, 13)

> It's all hot-dogs and burgers and chicken burgers and sometimes they do chicken wings and sausage rolls. There's a shop too and they do chocolate bars and jellies and fizzy drinks. (Josh, 13)

> Most people just eat rolls and crisps and bars. The shop upstairs, that's all they sell is sweets. They don't sell fruit or rolls and they sell fizzy drinks. Even if you wanted to stop taking them, even cut down on them, like they're still in front of you. (Anna, 15)

> The only thing you can really get is burgers, biscuits, chips, crisps and muffins. That's all people eat, they don't eat anything that would be good for you. (Sandra, 13)

> I don't eat that much good stuff for lunch. I just get a box of wedges or a sandwich. I like salads but it's easier to get junk food so it's too much hassle to try and have a healthy lunch every day. If you go to the shops there's not much of a choice to get good food. If you go up to get baps they're usually not very nice so it's just easier to buy hot food and have a good dinner I suppose. (Cian, 16)

Although a few of the teenagers said they would welcome healthy options, most bore testament to the popularity of junk food and fast food. Unlike the UK, where the Government is responsible for the food provided in schools, it is predominantly private tenders who do so in Ireland. Tenders to the schools I visited appeared to be supplying imperishable foods that promised flavour and fulfilment. The schools provided a constant flow of chips, burgers, hotdogs, sweets, bars, crisps and cakes and their students bought into these temptations. But they also knew the connection between consuming high calorie foods and gaining weight. The stigmatisation of overweight youths discussed in Chapter Four left many of those I spoke to battling a war between gratification and despair over eating certain foods.

The unregulated body: society's problem

Adolescents attain independence through taking responsibility for their own food intake, yet must do so within a regulated framework. Prominent theorists such as Foucault, Turner and Bordo have all commented on how the unregulated body is viewed as a problem for society. Foucault maintains that it is in the interest of society to ensure the regulation of bodies. Worked upon by discourse, every regulated body has social meaning inscribed upon it (1977). The monitored and controlled body becomes a display, invested with certain properties and inserted into regimes of truth through the operations of power and knowledge. As Foucault puts it:

> One must be concerned with the 'body politic', as a set of material elements and techniques that serve as weapons, relays, communication routes and supports for power and knowledge relations that invest human bodies and subjugate them by turning them into objects of knowledge. (Foucault, 1977:28)

According to Foucault, the unregulated body is a problem for social institutions. He holds that individuals normalise regulatory practices of their own bodies because they are constantly schooled in such practices through surveillance. The aesthetic-athletic body is put forward as a discourse of truth in popular press (see Chapters One and Two), where its prevalence acts as a form of surveillance, informing adolescents of the validated body form and monitoring their approximation to it. It is in the interest of popular press to promote the regulated body. Once people have internalised the feeling of being watched and begin to discipline themselves accordingly, asserts Foucault, the practice of disciplining becomes normal (1977). The mind becomes almost decentred from a complacent body which regulates itself out of habit. Chapter Six discusses how this understanding of regulation is actually a problem for the body. For now it suffices to say that bodies do not regulate themselves and even the most habitual regulatory practices demand mindful instruction. Despite shortfalls in Foucault's work, his notion of the unregulated body as a problem for society has been taken up by Bryan Turner and by Susan Bordo.

Turner does not refer specifically to either institution or discourse but rather formulates his own unique structure through which 'the problem of the body' can be understood (1984, 1992, 1996). He sees the representation of the external body within social space as largely to do with control of the internal body. If adolescents wish to exhibit a validated body externally, they have to control their desires and natural urges. As far back as the reformation, the threat of projecting an aura of idleness or lack of willpower was counteracted by the attainment of a controlled, 'dieted' body. 'Dieting, especially among the rich, was the main guarantee of health, mental stability and reason' (Turner, B., 1996:167). Turner notes that by the eighteenth century, George Cheyne became popular as a physician in London because he offered schooling on dietary regimes to the elite. Cheyne maintained that in order to sustain external status, internal regulation was required.

> If a Man has eaten or drank so much, as renders him unfit for the Duties and Studies of his profession, he has overdone it. Once a proper, regular diet has been established, the professional man has only two further requirements for sound health – (1) 'A Vomit, that can work briskly, quickly and safely' by cleaning, squeezing and compressing the knotted and tumified Glands of The Prima Viae', (2) 'Great, frequent and continued Exercise'. (Cheyne cited in Turner, B., 1992:189)

Certain practices of the eighteenth-century professional classes gradually percolated through the social system to all social groups in a pattern of organised eating, drinking and physical training (Turner, B, 1992:190). Adolescents who recognise the negative meaning placed by society on the unregulated body and wish to overcome this through regulation are confronting what is an old problem.

Discourses of truth have always targeted the regulation and control of natural bodily desires (see Chapter One). Turner draws on the work of Weber, the theorist of asceticism, to point to manifestations of the call for social control over natural bodily desires. In *The Protestant Ethic and the Spirit of Capitalism* (1965), Weber recounts how Protestantism prompted a rational ordering of the body which 'was thus protected from the disruptions of desire in the interests of continuous factory production' (Turner, B, 1984:100). European industrial capitalism, along with staunch Protestantism, was resolute about maximising efficiency of production so any natural desires which might threaten efficiency had to be controlled or denied. Even during early monastic Christianity, the natural flesh was a 'symbol of moral corruption which threatened the order of the world' (Turner, B, 1996:64). In an effort to avoid the social problems which liberated flesh might cause, 'the flesh had to be subdued by disciplines, especially by the regimen of diet and abstinence' (*ibid*). Protestantism and industrialisation, however, began to see the uncontrolled body less as a problem of religious righteousness for society and more as a problem for industrial production and utility. Common to both contexts was that unregulated bodies were condemned and the regulated body validated.

Today regulation often arises out of the problems which secular institutions such as the media and consumerism have with the unregulated body. Consumerism, the modern equivalent of the monastery, acts as a powerful discourse schooling individuals to 'get undressed – but be slim, good looking, tanned!' (Foucault, 1980:57). According to Turner:

> In a consumer culture, the body assumes a new social and individual significance. It becomes the site of personal strategies of health. jogging, slimming and keep-fit programmes are designed to promote health as the basis of the good life. (Turner, B, 1996:170-171)

Consumer culture persistently teaches individuals how bodies should be viewed: any 'softness of bulge comes to be seen as unsightly – as disgusting, disorderly' (Bordo, 1993:57). The bodies that society has no problem with are 'those that are tightly muscular or virtually skeletal' (*ibid*).

Turner and Bordo look mainly at regulation through dieting. Turner observes that it is through rejecting temptations that individual self-esteem is enhanced (1984:180; 1996:23, 170). Regulatory regimes are prompted by cultural expectations to fight fat and to resist consumer temptations. The adolescents described how they are continually surrounded by tempting foods. Bordo notes that it is socially acceptable for men but not women to give in to these temptations. The goal for women is to overcome the body's natural desire to be tempted: giving in to temptation makes for guilty eating (Bordo, 1993). Bordo argues that women are tempted to indulge in forbidden fruits and, given the huge range of new foods they can indulge in,

> ...the only way to win this no win game is to go beyond control, to kill off the body's spontaneities entirely – that is, to cease to experience hungers and desires. (Bordo, 1993:146)

Turner and Bordo both see the regulation of food intake as a rebellion against or rejection of natural desires in response to society's problem with the uncontrolled body.

The unregulated body: the individual's problem

Foucault, Turner and Bordo tend to focus on the problem of the unregulated body as social or structural whereas Goffman seeks to foreground the agent to some degree. Goffman's understanding of the problems individuals face in society when they have an unregulated body has been discussed in relation to stigma (Chapter Four). Goffman's focus is on how individuals manage their bodies in an attempt to overcome the problems they face in society. They are never invested with regulatory discourses from social structures. Goffman maintains that physical regulation is demanded not by structures such as the monastery, factory or shopping outlet, but rather by people themselves in their drive to attain validation within social interaction. Frost draws on Goffman's theory of the body as a means of understanding agency among young women.

> She is neither the victim of, for example, consumer capitalism and/or patriarchy and/or media pressure, nor the wilful perpetrator or 'own worst enemy' within the beauty system, but engaged in an interactive social process essential to identity formation, which she must engage with. (Frost, 2005:66-67)

However, while Goffman must be applauded for giving agency to the individual, he accords little to the body.

Frank achieves agency for the body by spinning on its head Turner's framework for bodily order within structure, emphasising the embodied agent rather than structure. Even Turner acknowledges Frank's criticisms:

> I moved theoretically downwards towards the body from the level of the societal, whereas an alternative and perhaps prior orientation would be to start with the body's problems for itself. He (Frank) argues that 'I propose instead to begin with how the body is a problem *for itself*, which is an action problem rather than a system problem, proceeding from a phenomenological orientation rather than a functional one'. (Turner, B., 1992:59)

Frank (1991) explores 'action problems' for the body in society, examining the 'mirroring', the 'communicative', and the 'dominating' body and the 'disciplining' body which deals with the problem of body regulation. He asserts that it is not social systems that regulate bodies, but bodies themselves. Regulation helps individuals cope with a sense of looking which they feel in relation to their bodies. Frank holds that disciplining regimes do not attempt to remedy the problem of lacking but try instead to 'forestall total disintegration' (Frank, 1991:55). Adolescents may view their bodies as somewhat lacking in relation to validated body forms, and the body copes with this through making itself predictable.

> With regard to control, the disciplined body makes itself *predictable* through its regimentation. So long as the regimen is followed, the body can believe itself to be predictable; thus being predictable is both the medium and the outcome of regimentation. (Frank, 1991:55)

The bodily regimes identified by Frank give a sense of control and order to the body. Through the body's own tasks it shields itself from the instability of total disintegration and deregulation. Frank gives the corporeal body credit for its work as an agent in protecting and producing itself.

Balancing temptation with regulation

The adolescents in this study discussed body regulation in terms similar to Frank's notion of making the body predictable (1991:55), rather than Turner's and Bordo's ideas of reaching beyond the body's hungers (Turner, 1984:180, 1996:23, 170; Bordo, 1993:146). By and large, they thought it acceptable to over indulge on occasion – it is not a problem so long as they compensate afterwards. They did not try to suppress their desires totally by adhering to rigidly ordered and regimented eating patterns. They admitted that they either lacked the willpower to do so or did not want to. They felt that they have natural desires which should be satisfied. Their compensation or 'regimentation does not remedy this lack, but it can forestall total disintegration' (Frank, 1991:55). The intention is to be able to indulge, even overindulge, but to be continually alert to the need to follow this by a counteracting regime which prevents plummeting into the realms of 'fat'. Adolescents' counteracting regimes were a process of balancing over indulgence and under indulgence so that they could get the best of both worlds.

> I eat loads of junk food. I prefer to eat all that sort of stuff but then you want to have a nice figure as well. You like to fit into your jeans after eating a packet of crisps or something. (Shannon, 14)

The teens felt it was acceptable to eat junk food – just as long as they enforced regulatory measures to prevent gaining weight. Some of them tried to flush high calorie foods out of their body after consumption.

> I eat junk food every day, but I balance it out. I have 2 litres of water every day and I walk to school so I usually don't find myself putting on too much weight and if I did find myself putting on weight, I'd just go easy on the junk food for the next few days. (Tara, 15)

> I try to drink eight glasses of water a day and jogging is now part of my routine because it's there. (Shauna, 16)

These adolescents generally accepted that they had natural desires which they wanted to satisfy through enjoying the tempting foods available. Regimentation was not an attempt to eliminate such desires but to counteract the fear of becoming fat.

Fat is associated with carelessness, laziness, repulsiveness and stupidity (see Chapter Four). These teenagers wanted to be able to indulge in tempting foods but since being fat was the primary cause of stigmatisation in schools they also dreaded getting fat. This fear was so great that some of them imagined irrational scenarios such as fat invading their body as if on an assigned mission over which they would have no control.

> The guy next door to me has put on a lot of weight. So I worry because I just don't want to turn out like that and I could. (Evan, 13)

It could happen any time. God knows what I'd do, probably collapse. Things like that frighten me to think I could get fatter and be afraid and paranoid all the time about what I'm eating. (Shauna, 16)

It's like a big fear for me; imagine you woke up really, really heavy one morning. It's a big thing. (Gillian, 16)

Becoming fat terrified many of the participants and they felt they had to employ regimes to counteract weight gain. They were victims of a situation where 'fighting fat is largely about seeking to display social fitness in a sizist culture, where manufactured intolerance is taken for granted and deemed healthful' (Monaghan, 2007:70).

If I found myself putting on weight I'd make a serious effort to get rid of it. I'd definitely do something about it if I was getting fat. (Cian, 16)

Even teens who stated that they ate what they wished and were not too concerned about their appearance admitted that they would not want to be fat. They sensed that if they gained weight, they would begin to experience feelings of guilt around their eating patterns and food choices.

Guilty eating

It was not eating but overeating that made these adolescents feel guilty. Guilt arose from feeling that they had overindulged. Of course 'overeating' is itself a subjective term, but guilty feelings could arise however they defined it. Bordo observes that men can eat shamelessly in public whereas women prefer to do so in private because they feel guilty about indulging. 'Cravings are a dirty, shameful secret, to be indulged in only when no one is looking' (Bordo, 1993:129). Gammon and Makinen also refer to women's eating as a naughty sexual secret (1994:151). For the girls I spoke to public eating was not such a shameful act. In these narratives, eating took place in public; it was regarded as a display of individual independence and a reason for social gatherings. As Shilling suggests:

Food continues to be used as a way of cementing and maintaining social relationships, and of demarcating certain relationships and identities as distinct and worthy of recognition and others as being low status and morally suspect. (Shilling, 2005:172)

Eating can provide a social communion for teenagers on which to mount friendships. Some of the youths talked about going down to the chipper or out for ice-cream in the evening to meet up with friends. They described how their guilt arose from overeating rather than public eating.

> I'd often meet up with my friends for chips or ice-cream in the evenings. I sometimes get something to eat as an excuse to meet up with my friends. I really enjoy it, but sometimes I do feel bad if I've already had my dinner and I feel like I'm after eating too much. (Mary, 13)

> Some weeks I go down with my friends and get a curry for five nights and I say 'that's enough I'm not getting any curries next week because I'm after treating myself too much. So I say 'I'll give myself a break this week and save up', because the amount of money that you spend on them is mad and you'd also feel like you were after putting on loads of weight and you have to get rid of it ... and you end up exercising more. (Anna, 15)

Both boys and girls regarded eating as a social occasion. The self-sufficiency involved in buying food showed their control over their intake. They enjoyed indulging together with friends. Guilt arose from a sense of having 'treated oneself too much' and necessitated regulatory regimes to 'forestall total disintegration' (Frank, 1991:55).

The intention behind the counteracting regimes described by the teenagers is vital: it is not to reject eating but to reject the consequences of overeating.

> If I eat loads I say 'Oh my God' and think I have put on pounds... but then I say 'oh that's ok. I'll get it off ... I'll do more exercise and it will be ok'. (Mary, 13)

> I keep on eating all the time, like I'm after having a big lunch and mum's making a stew this evening, I'll go home and eat the stew and after the stew I'd still be able to eat something else ... If I eat loads I feel like 'Oh my God what am I after doing, I'm just after eating too much'. You'd feel really annoyed with yourself. You feel like your stomach is all bloated and you feel full and it's not nice. I hate it. But it's like going to the gym, you feel like you can eat whatever you like before you go and then when you come out you feel like everything you're after eating is just gone. (Lynn, 16)

> When I'm going to the cinema I eat a huge thing of popcorn and sweets and coke and I come out feeling 'I really shouldn't have done that'. It puts a dampener on eating because you're feeling guilty, but you're also thinking 'oh my God it's only food'. So you say 'I shouldn't have eaten that much but now I'll do a hundred sit-ups'. (Gillian, 16)

The girls did not intend to reject or rebel against sinful public eating but rather to accept food, even embrace it, while rejecting fatness. They did not feel guilty before they ate but only when they felt they had overeaten. They thought it acceptable to eat what they wished, as long as they enforced regimes such as drinking plenty of water or exercising. The girls appeared to talk themselves through what they had done on occasions of perceived overeating and formulated the course of action to be taken to eradicate feelings of guilt. Bordo (1993) and Turner (1984, 1992, 1996) consider guilty eating common among females, but I found it just as common among the boys I spoke with.

Bordo gives an invaluable account of the dynamics involved in guilty eating but presents it as almost exclusively a female phenomenon, while men's eating as shameless. She describes a patriarchal setting where men are predominantly waited on, served and expected to consume 'Hungry Man Dinners' (Bordo, 1993:108). Men shamelessly eat man-sized meals, whereas guilt and shame prompt women to eat much less. Bordo notes the regulatory practices of men and women being united against 'a common enemy: the soft, the loose; unsolid, excess flesh' (1993:191). In Bordo's scenario, women lay the table with copious amounts of man-sized foods for their husbands. So although men are more independent than women, they have, in her view, little control over or input into their own eating practices.

Parental practices appear to be changing. The boys in this study mentioned their fathers preparing dinner and many of the boys took responsibility for providing their own lunches. They too were clear about the lure of treats and the guilt which followed overindulgence and the necessity to counteract this. The boys ate tempting foods as much as the girls did and perceived overeating as by no means shameless or guilt free. The over-fed body contradicts the aesthetic-athletic type body validated by adolescents and popular press for both sexes. Being fat had similar consequences for boys and girls (see Chapter Four). Their narratives largely confirmed the assertions of Gill, Henwood and McLean that 'discourse sets up the individual to discipline their own body, and finds them morally culpable if they fail' (2005:55). Both boys and girls were ridiculed and segregated if they failed, so it was not a fear of eating that drove counteracting regimes but a fear of failing to control fat.

> If I thought I was getting fat I'd kind of be annoyed with myself, I would be annoyed with myself and try and do a lot more exercise or even stop eating or something like that. (Kevin, 13)

> For the last two weeks I've been eating burgers every day as well as dinner. My dad cooks good stuff. I don't really mind about the last two weeks because I'm going to burn it off anyway, but if I were to sit around doing nothing then I probably would mind. I just ate them because I was hungry at the time and it was too much effort to go and get proper lunches. (Enda, 16)

> I've been eating so much rubbish and all lately and I have to try and get it all off again. I'm not starving myself but I was over-eating again but I'm not anymore. (Barry, 16)

> I really like sweets but I'm eating a lot of sweets and I'm trying to stop that now. I don't want to be fat when I get older. I just don't want to be big. If you want to be big, you want to be big with muscle rather than flab. (Evan, 13)

The boys continually described relationships with food similar to those described by the girls. They did not want to reject food but felt it necessary to maintain the body's predictability through compensating for perceived overeating. Some of them rationalised overeating in a form of self-talk and then formulated a counteracting response, just as the girls had done.

> If a girl would try to work off what she'd eaten then I suppose men would do that as well. I know that's what I'd do, go for a run or something to try to burn it all off. It's happened before if I'd gone out to breakfast with someone and I'd eaten loads and I'd think 'I shouldn't have done that.' Then at night time I'd go for a cycle or a run or something just to burn it off. Anyway it would make you feel better about what you'd done. If you sit around doing nothing you'll just feel awful but if you go out for a run or cycle you wouldn't feel as bad. You'd feel like you made an effort to get rid of it. (Cian, 16)

One young boy talked about overeating and then compensating but thought that boys might think it 'girlie' to talk openly about the need to compensate.

> When I eat too much I feel a bit bloated and full, I probably wouldn't eat any sweets the next day. Sometimes I might feel like I have to eat less the next day but then I might just say 'that was just a once off'. I'd just feel stupid and try to take a break from some stuff. I'd be afraid of the way I'd look if I kept eating like that. Some boys mightn't feel up to telling about how they feel, they don't want to say how they're overweight. They might think it's a bit girlie to say 'I'm going to stop because I don't want to get overweight'. (Ger, 13)

Ger does illuminate the preoccupation with restrictions on body talk that recurs so frequently in the boys' narratives. But it appeared to me that the boys spoke as openly as the girls about guilty eating and the need for counteracting regimens.

Normal or disordered counteracting regimes?

The teenagers' compensating regimes largely consisted of a spell of increased exercise or more monitored eating. Worryingly, however, some spoke of commonly using practices generally associated with eating disorders. The obsessive restriction of food that characterises anorexia nervosa may be simply a continuum of a modern dieting culture which views fat as a social problem (Turner, B., 1984, 1992). Anorexia offers a 'crystallisation' of wider regulatory practices in western society (Bordo, 1993) and is underpinned by the rejection of food and fat. However, the teenagers I spoke to wanted to reject only fat. Perhaps Bordo's account of bulimia is more in line with adolescent responses in that they generally wanted to consume food and enjoy it, but overeating was followed by guilt and a process of compensating.

> Bulimia precisely and explicitly expresses the extreme development of the hunger for unrestrained consumption (exhibited in the bulimic's uncontrollable food binges) existing in unstable tension alongside the requirement that we sober up, 'clean up our act', get back in firm control on Monday morning (the necessity for purge – exhibited in the bulimic's vomiting, compulsive exercising and laxative purges). (Bordo, 1993:201)

If counteracting regimes are aimed not at rejecting the body's valid desires but at forestalling totally succumbing to them (Frank, 1991), then the cyclical process adopted by these adolescents is not unlike bulimia. They embraced consumption, but unrestrained consumption could cause such panic and fear that vomiting became an accessible and desirable option. For youths who wish to enjoy all the temptations and pleasures within Baudrillard's 'hypermarket of culture' yet retain their embodied capital, bulimic regimes offer a perfect solution.

These teenagers knew many people who purged to retain the predictability of their body shape, proving it to be a practice common among more than just people with diagnosed eating disorders. Purging was used to empty the system so that it was okay to fill it again the next day.

> That's the way people do it, like if you're sick one day you'll eat the next. (Chloe, 13)

The girls described how purging was habitually used as a form of regulation in their communities and among their friends.

> When you eat loads like, you want to get sick. That's the way I feel but all the young girls down my way they get sick anyway, like when they eat stuff they take stuff for it and it makes them get sick so anything they eat they throw up afterwards. (Chloe, 13)

> More people are going on diets and more are sticking their fingers down their throat and all that. Because my friend was making herself sick there for a while and she's gone very thin. (Anna, 15)

> I wouldn't say to my friend to loose weight or anything because people do things to themselves if they think they're big. Some people take it the wrong way and make themselves sick. (Lynn, 16)

Bruch (1977) emphasises that eating disorders are more prevalent among middle-class girls with controlling parents, but all the narratives on bulimic behaviours referred to so far are taken from girls from working-class areas, and who described relationships with their parents as characterised by friendship rather than dominance. It appears that 'various lifestyle orientations must be considered open: youths with similar orientations do not all come from the same backgrounds' (Reimer, 1995b: 138).

What is startling about these narratives is that the girls described using counterating regimes for specific purposes and set periods of time to achieve a certain goal. They were chosen as quick fit solutions to regain equilibrium at times of self discomfort.

> The girl who lives next door to me, she's after having a baby, she keeps on taking Andrews and throwing up after she eats because she wants to get back skinny because she's only my height... She just wants her figure back. (Eve, 13)

> I did the throwing up your food thing and it wasn't nice. I did it for about three weeks... The first few times you do it you think 'oh great this is going to work' and after a while you realise all you're thinking about is food and throwing it up. You eat but then you're really, really hungry because your food isn't staying down... For a few days it was the best thing ever and then after a week it just made me feel sick because I'd been sick all the time. It is a sickness, it's

not something that's so glamorous but you know models do it. You know pop stars do it and in school I'd say a few are definitely doing it. (Shauna, 16)

Bulimic practice was referred to almost as aerobics might be. It was simply something the girls tried out for a while. I cannot say that they will not revert to vomiting as a regulatory practice in the future but for now it was simply a disciplining ritual chosen for a short time.

For some boys also, bulimic practice was a feasible option in achieving a specific goal. Although less normalised, the fact that they engaged in self-induced vomiting at all points to a change in who can be legitimately excluded from this debate. According to Monaghan, men are increasingly showing signs of damage in the war against fat. Eating disorders are rising among boys at the same time as obesity is rising (Monaghan, 2005:83). While the boys suspected that other boys purged, they were restricted in how openly this could be talked about.

> There's this guy in my class and last year, he was quiet chubby and he came back this year and he's thin. From what he said I'm pretty sure he would make himself get sick ... I don't think anyone would actually admit to it but I think some guys probably do it. (Enda, 16)

One boy explained how vomiting is normalised within certain sports. Again, it was used for a defined spell of time to attain some objective quickly.

> My friend does boxing so you have to keep to a particular weight. If they ate too much or weren't training and their weight went up, they'd make themselves sick for a while until they get it back again. It's like with jockeys too. (Barry, 16)

Barry points to the blurring of moderate and disordered forms of regulation in the quest for body validation. Whether for reasons of sport, peer acceptance, increased desirability or to combat the fear of fat, the adolescents' intention was to use vomiting to control and balance body size and forestall any threat of total disintegration (Frank, 1991:55). One boy who did not admit to using vomiting to control body size nonetheless described the use of purging when the equilibrium of the body is under threat.

> If I'm out and I'm after drinking loads and I have a feeling in my stomach too, then I get sick to get a lot of the alcohol up because the alcohol is going into

your liver, but if it's not digested, or whatever the stomach does to the alcohol, then it'll just be sitting in your stomach and mixing with everything so you just get the alcohol out of you and then you can go back to just being tipsy or whatever way you were before. (Rob, 16)

Many adolescents were not afraid of making themselves vomit – the alternative was far more frightening. What is most frightening, however, is that through the practice of purging, the disciplined and the diseased body are synthesised into one, leaving it almost impossible to identify where one ends and the other begins.

Conclusion

The analysis in this chapter of the teenagers' views indicates several contradictions as they try to attain or maintain a validated shape. They described being surrounded by an endless array of food marketing and choice and related how they associated sweets and chocolate with comfort and happiness and delighted in these temptations. They reported on the ready availability of such foods in their school tuck shops and vending machines. Many felt their schools offered little besides junk food and fast food. The food on offer contradicted the curriculum's message about the importance of eating healthy food. All were aware that the fast-fed body was severely stigmatised in their school and community, whereas the regulated body was habitually validated.

Theorists have explained the importance of body regulation: some view the unregulated body as a problem for society (Foucault, Turner, B., Bordo), others as a problem for individuals (Goffman) and the body (Frank) within society. Some theorists have suggested that regulation is an attempt to reject or overcome internal desires (Turner, B., Bordo) while others proposed that the purpose is not to overcome desires but to retain the body's predictability in the midst of them (Frank). The adolescents largely echoed Frank's outlook on body regulation. They found it exciting and indeed necessary to fulfil their desires for food, but felt that perceived overindulgence should be counteracted through compensating regimes, such as drinking more water, doing more exercise or monitoring their eating for a certain time.

It was predominantly the fear of becoming fat that prompted guilty eating. Both boys and girls reported feeling guilty after perceived overeating and discussed how they needed to follow certain regimes to regain bodily predictability and equilibrium after overindulging. This chapter has revealed the worrying extent to which counteracting practices such as purging were used by the adolescents and their peers. In many cases, the word 'vomiting' slipped nonchalantly into their normal vocabularies of body regulation, blurring the boundaries between discipline and disorder. These boundaries were remarkably fluid in the teenagers' stories of their quest for embodied validation through exercising also – as we see in Chapter Six.

6

Exercised Bodies

Introduction

The last chapter examined the complex contradictions adolescents have to deal with concerning indulgence and regulation of the body and their need to counteract indulgence and especially over indulgence. This chapter takes an in-depth look at working out – exercising and weight training – as an example of one activity for counteracting indulgence. Working out is greatly validating, as the narratives demonstrate. The youths learn about the validating nature of exercise and training from parents and siblings and at the gym. The theoretical subtleties which influence how we view adolescents' quests for validation are explored. The data demonstrate that validation must be understood as not just 'bodily' but 'embodied'. These teenagers pursue physical validation but this brings with it psychological validation. It is the 'lived body' (Merleau-Ponty, 1967), not a lifeless body, that seeks affirmation. Working out appears to have the power to affect the entire embodied individual in a distinctly validating way.

This chapter also reveals that while the visual results of working out offer embodied validation, so too can the activity itself. Simply working the body to accomplish physical goals and overcomes physical barriers can provide embodied validation in its own right.

Working out: social construction?

The theoretical work of Bourdieu and Giddens outlined in Chapter One and the theoretical approaches of Foucault, Turner, Bordo and Goffman referred to in Chapter Five can be used to illuminate the way in which working out validates embodiment.

The dual process of structure and agency that lies at the core of Bourdieu's concepts of 'habitus' and 'field' and Giddens' 'structuration theory' is useful for understanding adolescents' participation in exercise and weight training. These theories imply that on the one hand macro structures inform youths about the social meaning of body regulation, while on the other hand structures are maintained through each youth's micro participation in regulatory regimes. Foucault, Turner, and Bordo all generally follow the structural or macro aspect of dualism. Foucault argues in much of his work that structural or dominant discourses invest their knowledge in bodies so as to train, regulate and 'subjugate them by turning them into objects of knowledge' (Foucault, 1977:28). Turner sees the internal body as a site of desire which must be controlled by various regimens, arguing that 'the body of the individual is regulated and organised in the interests of population' (Turner, B, 1996:67). Similarly Bordo affirms that 'our bodies, no less than anything else that is human, are constituted by culture' (Bordo, 1993:142). So theories concerned with regulation as a requirement of society to ensure the stable production of itself, generally speak of the social construction of the body.

Other theorists have emphasised the role of individual agents in body regulation. For instance, Goffman holds that it is interaction with others which informs individuals on modes of self-regulation (1963a). Bodies are schooled not through imposed structures but through interaction. According to Goffman, individuals use this schooling to negotiate and enhance their social status and performances. A combination of both aspects of dualism has underlined much of the data explored in this book. For example, the adolescents recognise that they are schooled by popular press on which bodies types are validated. However, validation is much more meaningfully negotiated and assigned at the level of interaction with embodied peers (see Chapter One). Similarly, the adolescents knew the social meaning associated with the fat body through its rejection by popular press but learned about the intricacies of coping with being fat through interaction with peers (see Chapter Four).

Goffman's work differs from much writing on the sociology of the body because it does not focus on the body as 'the intersection between the self and society, but on the interactively produced social self as a presentation or performance' (Frost, 2005:65). Rather, self presentations and performances are influenced by a social 'interaction order' or 'shared vocabularies of body idiom' (1963a, 1967). Vocabularies of body idiom, like Giddens' notion of language, are enabling. They provide a medium through which individual bodies are enacted and validated. From Goffman's perspective, these adolescents may work out to improve their everyday presentations and performances among their peers and acquaintances. They exercise and train for the betterment of the individual rather than for the good of the population. Yet the teenagers are still following social rules and for this reason Goffman's body may be placed also within the realm of social constructionism (Shilling, 1993, 2003).

Whether teenagers work out because of schooling from dominant discourses or intimate interactions, their stories demonstrate that they receive influential information on body validating activities, such as exercise and weight training.

Working out: schooling from parents

The adolescents spoke of how the views of siblings and parents on working out influenced how they valued exercising and weight training. Schooling on exercise and training techniques took place predominantly at the interactive level (Goffman) of the family. The significance of exercising may have infiltrated through from popular exercise practices in dominant discourses (Foucault, Turner, Bordo). However the adolescents were most convinced about exercise when they saw how it enabled family members. Whether due to discourse or interaction or both, it was always the aesthetic-athletic type body that the teens referred to as enabling.

Body regulation among adolescents has frequently been connected to their parental relationships. Both Turner (1984, 1992) and Bordo (1993) draw on the work of Bruch (1977) who asserts that body regulation through dieting primarily affects middle-class girls from over-protective families (also Chernin, 1983; Orbach, 1988; Gordon, 1990, 2001; Frost, 2005). Anorexia is seen in political terms as a rebellion against maternal care and a quest for autonomy – a rebellious protest which ultimately leaves young girls trapped and powerless within their practices of asceticism. For the adolescents I spoke to, regulation emerged from quite different relations with parents. Parents and teenagers schooled each other on regulatory regimes of the body. Rather than regulation being an act of rebellion, it was more an act of imitation or even competition. The adolescents were not pursuing solitary asceticism; they and their parents were on a shared pursuit of aestheticism and athleticism.

Bruch (1977) focuses on hierarchical tensions within mother-daughter relationships whereby teen body regulation is an act of resistance. However, the girls I interviewed reported relationships with their mothers that were based on friendship. It was in many cases their mother's opinion of her own body and her perceived need to regulate it which made the girls feel they should do so too. The girls sometimes compared their body to their mother's. Mothers who took the same size clothes as their daughters often spoke about needing to trim down and shape up. This had a profound impact on the teenage daughter's sense of self and made her feel she needed to copy her mother or compete with her.

> When she [mother] put on weight she said 'I'll reduce food and keep fit'. Then I think I have to loose weight. (Mary, 13)

> When she's [mother] talking about her weight I'd say 'I'm fat as well so' and she'd say 'no you're not' ... She already had the slender-tone belt that she bought about two years ago before she went on holidays and she found that really good ... so she bought the shorts the other day. Because of her bad back she can't do as much exercise as I do but we kind of encourage each other. (Gillian:16)

Exercise bound mothers and daughters. They schooled each other on effective activities in their shared pursuit of validation.

> I'd do that in my house every night, you know get out of the bath and do a few sit-ups. Like all the time, if I was in the house with my mam we'd do sit-ups together. I love doing exercises and I do have my little sister doing them now. She's only ten. I guess my mam influences me the way that she is. Yeah because she does be messing and she'd say 'will you hold my feet and I'll do a few exercises, sit-ups?' And then I'd say 'you hold my feet now and I'll do a few'. I think it's good and it doesn't take long because you feel much better in yourself when you do exercise. (Lynn, 16)

Although exercising is clearly an individualised activity with individual goals, interactive practices helped this mother and daughter to fulfil their goals. Lynn felt 'much better in herself' after exercising, indicating how she was psychologically more validated through the worked out body – a point to which I return later.

Some boys mentioned that they were influenced by the weight training regimes of their older brothers which helped attain an appearance of superior body strength. This influenced their choice of what training to partake in themselves. The younger boys knew that weight training can stunt growth but were impressed by how attaining an athletic physique had enabled their siblings. They discussed how working out helped their older brothers to overcome stigmatisation through altering their body dimensions and definition. Both boys and girls learned the value of working out first hand through daily interaction with siblings and parents, and noted that siblings often emulated their parents' exercising and that parents facilitated and encouraged their children to work out. Parents did not want to be fat and warned their children against getting fat. The teens largely correlated working out with increased confidence and happiness – increased validation.

> I see my brother and he wants to get stronger, like more muscle and he always weighs himself to see what weight he is, every morning ... He wants gym membership so he can get stronger because my parents have gym membership. He wasn't very confident but now he is. (Evan, 13)

> One brother weighed eighteen stone and he was really unhappy with himself so he's gone down to sixteen stone now. My dad lost weight too. He did weights and ran. He's happy now and he's keeping it that way because that's healthier. I don't do any weights or press-ups yet. I do sit-ups. I do fifty every second day. (Mark, 12)

> I do dancing, about five or six hours a week. I used to train at swimming, because I'm a lifeguard, about four hours a week but now I only do one. I do a lot of walking as well. I walk to school and I walk home from school and I walk to work and home ... If I was just sitting there I might start doing sit-ups as well. We have weights and all in our house and I started them. My brother has a boxing thing so I do that too. He's a fitness instructor. My brother and my dad do weights too. Dad's big into it so that's where my brother gets it from. (Caoimhe, 16)

> My brother doesn't like putting on weight so he goes to the gym to get it back off. He works in an office and he does a competition every so often with a lot of lads to see how much weight they can loose in a certain amount of time.

They just try to take off weight and then they weigh themselves on a certain day and whoever has lost the most weight wins. They put on bets with each other and whoever wins the competition wins the money. To lose weight he'd go to the gym more often. Sometimes he goes for runs. (Kevin, 13)

My brother says 'you should go running with me' ... He runs up to the park and runs around it and runs back down because he's real fit. He comes back home at about nine o'clock; he goes running round the flats again, he runs up and down the steps ... None of my brothers would like to be fat because you know if they see someone going by and they're fat, they say 'oh look at him'. Even my mum does it. She's that bad, say she saw a big girl or a big boy going by she'd say 'if you ever got like that I'd kill you'. (Eve, 13)

My brother is not fat but he used to be and my mother got him out walking and jogging. He goes jogging with me, once a week for an hour. I do a half hour walk each day and sit-ups and stretches. (Shauna, 16)

Their parents' views about exercise and training clearly influenced what regulatory practices the teenagers and their siblings thought worthwhile. All were in pursuit of a fit, firm athletic physique, whatever their age or sex.

The idea of working out as a counteracting regime was perpetuated by parents. Many of the participants who described their parents' interest in exercise were the same youths as talked about regularly going out for family dinners and treats, as in Baudrillard's 'hypermarket of culture' (1982) where people seek to enjoy and experience everything. Here, parents balance experiences of physical indulgence with the need for regulation. And the use of exercise equipment to regulate signifies further indulgence.

Working out: schooling in the gym

The gym may be viewed as a site of both consumer status and self-commitment (Bordo, 1993; Mansfield and McGinn, 1993; Fussell, 1994; Wacquant, 1995; Monaghan, 1999; Sassatelli, 2000 and Crossley, 2004, 2005, 2006). It has become highly visible as the site where the toned body is produced, and gym activities are increasingly portrayed and glamorised in popular media (Sassatelli, 2000:227). The official age at which youths can access gyms is not always made clear. Some of the teenagers in this study were able to bypass the age restrictions and others were admitted if accompanied by their parents. Otherwise they resorted to creating a personal mini-gym.

Two hundred and forty two adolescents were asked to comment in open-ended question and answer sheets on the exercise regimes they partake in, if any. The younger girls described regulation through participation in team sport and individualised exercise regimes such as sit-ups, walking and running. The older girls, however, indicated that participation in team sport is overwhelmingly replaced by sole participation in individualised exercise in later adolescence and many named the gym as essential for exercising. The few younger girls who reported using treadmills and exercise bikes did so at home, not in gyms. Amazingly, some of the younger boys did mention using exercise and weight programmes at a gym. Many boys who did not or could not access formal gyms invested in their own fitness sanctuaries at home.

The cost of exercise equipment is no longer beyond many self-sufficient teens. Consumer outlets also invite parents annually to purchase gym toys such as mini-treadmills and weightlifting benches as Christmas gifts for children as young as four. The notion of kids' gyms is moving from the US to Europe. They are purpose built for working out with equipment cut down to size. Eight-year-old Luke, a member of the 'Next Generation Club' in Britain, confesses 'I come to the gym after school and at the weekends. My favourite part is the weights. I exercise for 40-50 minutes and I think I'm getting fitter' (quoted by Hill, *The Observer*, Oct 2003). Whether striding in the gym, running on the track or doing push-ups in his own bedroom, Luke represents a reality where working out through individualised training is no longer only for adults.

Gyms educated the teenagers who attended them on effective modes of body regulation. They had already learned the value of working out from parents and siblings and felt encouraged to join gyms when they heard feel-good stories from parents and siblings and when they recognised bodily improvements. The value of working out was reinforced at the gym, although in a different way. According to the teenagers, people who attend gyms rely much more on bodily (unfocused interaction) than verbal communication (focused interaction) (Giddens, 1991).

Crossley found in his research on gyms that people at some moments are totally consumed by exercise, while 'at others they are more concerned with catching up with gossip or a joke' (2004:56). Coming together to exercise can create bonds, friendships and intimacies among individuals who would otherwise remain strangers (Crossley, 2004, 2006). Similarly, Leeds Craig and Liberti noted that the arrangement of the equipment shifted the focus from exercising to conversation and sociability (2007:684). However, it is in group exercising classes, such as circuit training (Crossley, 2004), gymnastic exercise (Sassatelli, 2000) or GetFit Clubs (Leeds Craig and Liberti, 2007) that friendships are likely to develop. Machine training, on the other hand, requires individualised time and 'the continuation of the exercise relies on the capacity of each client to isolate from others and to focus on a personal sequence of movements' (Sassatelli, 2000:232).

The adolescents who went to gyms were taught that working out demanded concentration and no distractions.

> There's no real atmosphere in the gym. No one's really laughing and going around, it's all just everyone keeping to themselves, nice and quiet and focused. A few people would be talking, but they wouldn't be talking loud. There's music in the background and that would be about it. (Enda, 16)

> No one really talks to each other, you just go and do your own thing. There's people there and they want to get in shape so they're just concentrating on that. They don't want to stop and start talking, they just want to keep on going at it. (Cian, 16)

According to those who attended the gym there was little verbal interaction, yet the detail of their narratives indicates much bodily interaction. Just as the regulatory regimes of family members offered adolescents a form of schooling on disciplining techniques, so too did the strangers they met at the gym. Once inside it was not the posters of ideal bodies on walls that the teens spoke of, but their symbolic interaction (Goffman, 1963a, 1967) with other gym-goers. On the one hand, the settings they depicted were highly social in that bodies educate other bodies on working out and display the tangible proof of it. On the other hand, they were highly individualised in that gym-goers seemed reflexively bound to the task for which they had come. Their stories indicated how 'the disciplined body may be among others, but it is not with them' (Frank, 1991:55).

There are not a lot of people talking. There's just music playing. Most people just keep to themselves ... Everyone's taking it seriously and some people might listen to music and others watch TV and when I go to the university gym there's a TV at each treadmill. When I was there last week there was a girl walking and when I looked at her treadmill she was walking for an hour and ten minutes just watching the TV. Some people are just freaks for fitness. You get the ones who are just walking and walking and walking and walking. Then you see guys pushing the weights. Huge guys pushing huge weights and they're just doing it to get a big physique. You see them all because there's lots of mirrors around. Around the whole place there's a lota, lota mirrors. There are no posters or anything which I thought you would see, of body-builders and advertising, but they're not there at all. (Andy, 16)

Nobody talks. You see women going around in twos but a lot of people don't even talk in the changing rooms. It's like they're saying 'I'm here to achieve a goal and I'm going to get it'. It's very intense. People are trying to do so much to be fit and toned ... It's really intense. You see people on the bikes or the strider and they're so determined looking and they're sweating. There'd be people there practically all night ... There are people who would spend three hours up there. They'd lift weights, go on the treadmill, do the bike, steps, go down for a swim, go into the Jacuzzi and then the steam room afterwards, like the sauna. It's like a religion; they think they have to do it. (Gillian, 16)

Many of Crossley's gym-goers were motivated to attend the gym because of the prospect of 'having a laugh' or wanting 'human contact' (Crossley, 2006:37). These youths viewed the gym as sites where verbal interacting and bonding was frequently frowned upon because it distracted from the primary intention of working out. The teens and fellow gym-goers were expected to 'concentrate on the exercise of his or her own body, moving it, observing it', while 'exposing it to the gaze of others as prescribed by the demands of the exercise' (Sassatelli, 2000:235). They communicated with each other through mirrors and glances. Messages on working out were sent through the visual aesthetic-athletic proof of individualised labouring.

Working out: embodied construction?

Viewing the body as a social construction can be useful for understanding how discourses (Foucault) or shared interactive vocabularies (Goffman) provide schooling on body techniques. However, it can be problematic to emphasise the social construction of the body over and above the corporeal construction of the body.

Foucault suggests that external forces continually construct bodies through mindful duress (1977). He describes how panoptic surveillance caused prisoners to be aware of being watched by prison guards at random moments and how not knowing precisely when this was made them regulate their bodies and behaviour all the time. Body regulation techniques did not emerge from external threat or coercion, but from acquired, internalised modes of operation (McNay, L, 1992:35). Once the feeling of being watched had been internalised and the prisoners had disciplined themselves accordingly, the practice of disciplining simply became normal (Foucault, 1977). There is a sense that these prisoners' minds become decentred from complacent bodies that regulate themselves out of habit. Bodies seemingly self-regulate to the beat of familiar institutional signals, regimes and timetables. Time measured and paid must 'be a time without impurities or defects; a time of good quality, throughout which the body is constantly applied to its exercise' (Foucault, 1977:151). The body becomes merely a decentred machine where 'discipline is no longer simply an art of distributing bodies, of extracting time from them and accumulating it, but of composing forces in order to obtain an efficient machine' (Foucault, 1977:164). According to Foucault, when regulation is standard behaviour the body almost instantaneously polices itself, as a machine would, without any need for conscious instruction.

Foucault truly describes the body as a social construction, where social discourses normalise their power within bodies. For Foucault's body, discourses have 'an immediate hold upon it; they invest it, mark it, train it, torture it' (Foucault, 1977:25). He takes as an example the soldier, as someone born with certain attributes but who

> ...by the late eighteenth century, has become something that can be made; out of a formless clay, an inapt body, the machine required can be constructed; posture is gradually corrected; a calculated constraint runs slowly through each part of the body, mastering it, making it pliable, ready at all times, turning silently into the automatism of habit; in short, one has 'got rid of the peasant' and given him 'the air of a soldier'. (Foucault, 1977:135)

Much of Foucault's work neglects how conscious motivation, choice and instruction must be present for even the most habitual tasks. It is almost impossible to view adolescents' bodies as objects of discipline that simply comply with regulatory discourses. Foucault's position changes in his later volumes, where he pays attention to individual agency and the material body. However, problems of discursive reductionism characterise the most popular developments of Foucault's analysis (Shilling, 2005:72).

While Foucault gives society responsibility for constructing the body, Frank acknowledges that construction is the responsibility of the body itself. Frank's corporeality is inhabited by a centred mind that depends on the body to carry out tasks. 'Bodies alone have 'tasks'. Social systems may provide the context in which these tasks are defined, enacted, and evaluated, but social systems themselves have no 'tasks" (Frank, 1991:48). These tasks allow agents to cope with a sense of lacking and to make the body predictable. The corporeal body is given credit for its work as an agent in protecting and producing itself. It is only the body that can carry out these tasks. Social systems merely provide the context in which tasks are understood (*ibid*).

Crossley, like Frank, emphasises individual corporeal responsibility for the construction of the body (2001, 2004, 2005, 2006). According to Shilling, Crossley's resurrection of the body within social thinking 'was timely as it coincided with a growing feeling that while theories of the body illuminated the *Korper* (the structural, objectified aspects of physical being), they had yet to come to grips fully with the *Leib* (the living, feeling, sensing, and emotional aspects of bodily experience)' (Shilling, 2003:204).

Crossley provides a detailed account of how the body carries out tasks to construct and modify itself through 'reflexive body techniques' (RBTs) (2004, 2005, 2006). RBTs are the 'body techniques whose primary purpose is to work back upon the body, so as to modify, maintain or thematize it in some way' (Crossley, 2005:9). This working back upon the body may involve one or two agents. Firstly, one body may work upon the body of another, for instance in hairdressing. Secondly, RBTs can involve one single body working back upon itself (2005:10); for instance, adolescents may jog to burn fat or lift weights to tone up. Even though these RBTs can become habitual, they always require a centred mind. 'Agents fairly regularly find themselves discussing ... their reasons for carrying on' (Crossley, 2006:36). Therefore, for Crossley, even habitual regulation requires motivation, whereas for Foucault it requires unquestioned compliance.

Reflexive body techniques explain how working out is fundamentally about working on the body and working with the body. Importantly, both Crossley and Frank take the view that working out encompasses both mind and body, making the body that emerges an embodied construction, rather than a social construction. Embodied individuals construct themselves through co-dependence between mind and body. Working out impacts back upon the body through physical modification (Crossley, 2004:38). Working out also impacts back up on the mind (sometimes irrespectively of changes in appearance) to boost self-esteem and confidence (Crossley, 2006:42). In both ways the body proves and validates its own construction and worth.

Validation through *working on* the body

Through exercise and training the body works back upon itself to make it predictable. This is particularly important where predictability is undermined by messages to eat indulgently yet look good. However, the worked out body has the power to communicate more than just consistency, as it is concerned with body shape as well as weight. The athletic body exhibits its labouring through definition and exhibits its control through alteration, providing tangible validation of achievements and worth. For many of the young people I spoke to, embodied construction through exercise regimes such as sit-ups was essential because they provided visual proof of being toned.

> I do about thirty sit-ups a day because I want a flat stomach and they just work their way into your routine. (Shauna, 16)

> I do sit-ups and push-ups and crunches to be toned. (Eoin, 13)

> I think the stomach and the legs are the most important for a girl ... They do sit-ups and press-ups to keep their stomach toned and keep their legs a nice shape. That's what I do anyway and it's great when you see it working. (Shannon, 14)

Visual proof of bodily changes gave the adolescents psychological as well as physical validation. They felt proud when they worked out. It made them feel 'better' or 'good' about themselves, bringing a sense of achievement.

> If I didn't do them [sit-ups] I wouldn't feel right, like I have to do them. I feel better with myself if I do them because I think my stomach is going down. I'm

after doing my exercises. It makes you feel better in a way if you see that it's flattening. (Anna, 15)

You just feel better about yourself when you feel like you've worked out. If you sit there all day and do nothing there's no sense of accomplishment. (Cian, 16)

I'd lie on my bed when I'm watching TV and I'd be just doing sit-ups and each day I'd probably do more of them ... I'd increase it because if you start low you become fit and you feel good about yourself. If you're just lazing on the couch all the time you don't feel that nice ... If I was tired after thirty I'd maybe take a little rest but then I'd go back and do the next twenty. You like to aim your target at whatever number and get that far. You feel good about yourself if you do. (Shannon, 14)

The youths described how physical changes allowed them to witness the fruits of their labouring and how this validated them psychologically as well as physically. They indicated that psychological validation was not dependent only on physical changes, however (Crossley, 2006:42), but was also achieved through the sense of self-worth attained from simply working out and becoming proficient on exercise machines.

Validation through *working* the body

Participants who attended gyms talked about the feeling of self-worth that came from pushing the body against the ferocity of exercise machines. Working out on machines was motivated by two things. Firstly, enhanced self-worth came from altering or maintaining the body ('forestalling disintegration', Frank, 1991). The body worked back on itself to modify or maintain itself (Crossley, 2005:9). Here the adolescents were concerned with the visual aspect of the body – the body-project (Giddens, 1991).

Secondly, they were motivated by the satisfaction that came from this body work. They were concerned with body action as much as body construction. According to Crossley:

Theorists fail to consider the pleasures and purposes of body work at the level of the lived body, the social nature of some forms of working out and the sense of self that attaches to certain forms of bodily doing, as opposed to bodily looking; this is, to the fact that running around for an hour or pushing weights can restore an agent's sense of their self and agency intrinsically, whatever it's wider consequences. (2006:47)

For the teenagers, agency came through working the body, as well as working on the body. Exercise machines validated the working body through providing tangible numerical proof of calories burnt, distances achieved, speed attained etc.

> I can't see why you can't get as much enjoyment out of walking the dog. When I was on the treadmill I was thinking that I should be walking Cindy instead of walking on the treadmill. I felt kind of guilty but if I went walking the dog I wouldn't feel that I had achieved anything because you wouldn't know how many calories you'd burnt. That's really important because it's in front of you all the time on the treadmill and all of a sudden that's all you're looking at. You're just looking at the numbers going up and you're saying 'keep going'. (Gillian, 16)

Gym machines provide quantified, scientific proof of body work. The teens placed great emphasis on numerical validation of their body work and believed that the higher the numbers, the higher the validation.

> I'm on the treadmill and there's loads of buttons and you can press each one. Really it's just as fast as I can go. I'd get on it and you know the way it goes real fast, I'd try to keep up with it as fast as I can go. Even if I got tired I'd go and do something else but I'd always come back to the walking thing. I think that's the best one you can do and your legs start getting real tired but I just keep on going like I time it and I say 'no I have to do it' and you do feel like just collapsing. I always do that. (Lynn, 16)

> Even if I was tired I'd keep going because if you set a goal for yourself and not accomplish it then you'll feel terrible. You think 'I can't accomplish the things I set out to do, even the small things, giving an extra minute isn't going to make that much difference to me'. If you want to do a twenty minute jog or something and you're after running for nineteen and then with one minute to go if you don't do the extra minute then you've wasted nineteen minutes and you're going to have to do it again another day. (Rob, 16)

> I got up on the treadmill and I said 'I'll do a hundred' and I ended up burning a hundred and fifty calories because every time I got to the next ten I was thinking 'keep going now, keep going'. I felt I had to keep going until I eventually got a stitch and had to stop. My friend was on the one beside me and she was running and running and running and I was walking really fast but she only burnt half the amount of calories I did. Basically I was thinking if I burn more I'll loose more weight and I want to be toned. I don't want big flabby thighs. I just wanted to keep going, burn another ten, another ten and

then just five more but eventually just had to stop because I couldn't do any-more. My body had to tell me to stop. I had to get a stitch. So my body just had to say 'listen Gillian stop', like that's what it was doing by getting a stitch. I then had to tell myself 'look you're dying with a stitch you have to stop' but I probably would have kept going and kept going until I did get a stitch in the end. Then my friend stayed on for another few minutes because she was like 'no I have to get to a hundred, I have to get to a hundred'. She felt also that she had to get higher and higher. (Gillian, 16)

These narratives provide astounding insights into the embodied nature of working out. They reveal the role of the mind in this process and chal-lenge Foucault's assertion that the body can come to regulate itself almost instantaneously (1977). Comments such as 'I have to do it' or 'keep going now, keep going' signify how routines of body regulation are driven by centred, mindful instruction. Foucault focuses on the body as an objec-tive machine (1977:135) whereas Crossley focuses on how the body understands machines in the practical and embodied sense of enjoying mastery over them and points out that 'the purpose of these machines is only ever accomplished with the compliancy of the agent' (Crossley, 2004: 50). Crossley's gym-goers had a repertoire of motives that they drew upon to persuade themselves to 'make the effort' of going to the gym (2006:36). My gym-goers had a repertoire of mindful instructions they used to push their body to work while at the gym.

These narratives also emphasise the role of the corporeal aspect of em-bodiment in working out. The gym-goers mentioned how they 'get real tired' or 'were absolutely exhausted'. Here the body is a real feeling and sensing entity in its own right, that is not always entirely compliant. The role of the corporeal was further exemplified by Gillian, who imagined that by giving her a stitch her body was trying to tell her: 'listen Gillian stop'. Even if the adolescents lost consciousness of their body work during the workout, the body was discovered in moments of exhaustion and aches (Crossley, 2006) – it 'reappeared' (Leder, 1990). Regardless of their levels of fitness, they knew that the body would make its own capabilities and limits known through tiredness, cramps and pains. Nonetheless, they felt that challenging those limits was intrinsic to feeling more validated through working out.

Machines proved to the adolescents the extent of their body work, and so too did the feeling of muscular aches, tension and relaxation. In the course of everyday life people often try to economise on effort and energy, avoiding pain and exhaustion if they can, yet people frequently frame the aches and pains of working out in a positive light (Crossley, 2006:39). Stress and tiredness often signify the need for exercise as exercise can flush them out. Gym-goers come to 'reframe muscular 'burn', stiffness, breathlessness, a pounding heart and exhaustion as both intimate pleasures ... and as signs of achievement and well-being' (Crossley, 2006: 40). The same applied to the adolescents in this study, who viewed exercise as a means of overcoming feelings of laziness and aches and as a way of gauging the body's mastery over exercising activities.

> If I don't do exercises I'd feel like I was getting lazy and I'd be real disappointed. When you do exercise those pains that you get from exercising just go away because you're getting used to it and that just makes you feel great about yourself and what you can do. (Lynn, 16)

> I set myself a goal and then I make a higher goal for myself, running or something. It makes me feel good about myself that I'm doing it and not just lazing around. And even if you are tired, your muscles would be aching but you'd have the energy to do it... If I'm not too tired I'll just really push myself because it makes me feel I've done something and I'm proud of myself that I actually did it. (Barry, 16)

> The first couple of times I went to the class I was so stiff the next day and for a few days but you get used to it and your body begins to work better for you... I usually feel so good when I come out of the class. It's like 'yahoo'. I've burnt a couple of calories and you feel like you really achieved something, (Gillian, 16)

> I'd just do push-ups and these things that tense up all the muscles along your abs ... It's like if you work your muscles you kind of get this buzz afterwards like you're really relaxed. You're not tense because you feel you've done something and you know it because you feel your muscles relaxing. You can say to yourself 'that was good'. (Rob, 16)

Many of the youths talked about the importance of feeling the work of the body. Feeling muscles contract and relax, tense and release, made the adolescents 'feel proud', 'feel good' or 'feel a buzz'.

Their goals when working out were wholly self-assigned. Some used working out as a way of proving they were in control. They could 'turn off' other demands playing on their consciousness (Crossley, 2006:43). Body-builder Sam Fussell notes that for him training was a way to escape external demands.

> The gym was the one place I had control. I didn't have to speak, I didn't have to listen. I just had to push or pull. It was so much simpler, so much more satisfying than life outside. I regulated everything ... It beat the street. It beat my girlfriend. It beat my family. I didn't have to think. I didn't have to care. I didn't have to feel. I simply had to lift. (Fussell, cited in L. Wacquant 1995:165)

According to Elliot and Lemert, survival within globalisation demands that individuals seek personal solutions to social problems in the hope of shutting out uncertainty and disappointment (2006:9). People generally set their own goals and agendas for working out. They make promises to themselves about the amount of body work they need to do to experience pride and success. Failure to complete promised body work often results in feeling disappointed with themselves.

> It's like with jumping [high jump] it makes you feel like you're accomplishing something. Like if you set a goal for yourself and say 'I want to do the highest one' and you go for it, it makes you feel really good. But if you kind of say you don't want to do the highest one and then rather than working at it you let the opportunity pass you by, if you don't take every opportunity, you can feel like you haven't accomplished what you set out to do and you feel like you're not as good a person, not in personality, but that you can't stick to your own word to yourself. (Rob, 16)

The teenagers described how working out accommodated body construction and body action – both of them validating activities. They felt pride and accomplishment in working the body and working on the body. Their bodies represented a space where they could obtain control and predictability, since 'regularised control of the body is a fundamental means whereby a biography of self-identity is maintained' (Giddens, 1991:57). It is 'crucial to the sustaining of the individual's protective cocoon in situations of day-to-day interaction' (Giddens, 1991:56). Many of these youths relied on regularised body work to maintain their self-identities and protect their self-worth.

Conclusion

Much of the prominent literature on the sociology of the body has focused on a social constructionist view of the body, in which the body is regulated because regulation is in the interests of, and dictated by, society (Foucault, Turner, Bordo). Other literature has adopted a more agentic standpoint, explaining body regulation as being in the interests of individuals who interact in society (Goffman). In both instances the body is influenced by social rules and rituals. However, we must understand the body as never constructed by such rules and rituals. They merely give individuals a form of schooling on body regulation.

This chapter has focused on the home and the gym as two areas where the teenagers are educated on the value of working out. The participants and their parents encouraged and even competed with each other with their exercising and training. They spoke of frequently working out with their parents in a friendly way. They schooled each other on techniques that could enhance size and definition. Parents discouraged their children from gaining weight and both they and their offspring appeared to be in common pursuit of aestheticism and athleticism.

These teenagers received a message that working out enhanced status. The children of parents who had gym membership or exercise equipment in the home were eager to participate in similar activities. They heard feel-good stories about the gym from their parents and siblings and saw that perceived improvements in body tone, definition, shape, strength etc were enabling for them. The aesthetic-athletic body spoke through its visible presence. Those who accessed gyms found that induction into working out was done largely through non-verbal bodily communication rather than verbally.

Parents, siblings and the gym educated teenagers on the body but did not construct or regulate bodies: bodies have ultimate responsibility for their own regulation (Frank, Crossley). This view recognises the corporeality of the body as an agent in body regulation, construction and action. The teenagers also emphasised the role of the mind in these processes. At no point did they suggest that their bodies regulate themselves once regulation is normalised (Foucault, 1977). They talked about the importance of mind centred motivation, choice and instruction, thus understanding working out as entirely embodied. Body techniques worked back upon the body and worked back upon the mind (Crossley), validating both. The adolescents told me about the sense of achievement they got from witnessing the fruits of physically *working on the body* and also from *working the body.*

They spoke about how they educated themselves about the muscular and cardiovascular capabilities of their own corporeality through working out. Validation emerged from challenging the body's limits – feelings of muscular tension and exhaustion, followed by relaxation and jubilation. Setting personal goals and overcoming the physical and psychological barriers to achieving them gave them a great sense of control. They relied on body work for a feeling of validation which was reaffirming both physically and psychologically.

7

Schooled Bodies

Theoretical discussions about physical bodies seldom present the subjects' own realities and ideas, especially when they are children and adolescents. This book gives a detailed account of how adolescents negotiate a sense of body and embodied validation. It takes readers into the worlds of thirty youths and their embodied stories that shift between happiness and heartache. It illustrates the value of in-depth research which eschews generalisation in favour of individual narratives. The stories in this book pinpoint precisely how teenagers are schooled on the body by popular press, peers and parents and how this shapes the way they regard their own bodies.

The role of popular press

The adolescents in this study regarded popular press as pivotal to how they came to understand the body shape and size they should strive for. With their changing corporeality and shifting social roles, they viewed press and advertising as evidence of the bodies that are expected and acceptable in society today. The media assigns a status of validation to certain bodies, and schools onlookers on how to attain this status and the growing resources that accompany it. Beautiful, fulfilled, assured celebrity bodies dominate popular press. Many of the girls talked about celebrities adoringly and with longing, while boys talked about their physical qualities and successfulness. They focused on an aesthetic-athletic body, the type of body the popular press promotes.

The aesthetic-athletic body acts as a discourse of truth (Foucault, 1980) promising increased personal and social benefits for those who possess it. Just as bodily asceticism was once validated through its association with salvation (Foucault, 1977) and bodily efficiency through its association with economic success (Weber, 1965), so today bodily aestheticism and athleticism are validated because of the personal and social benefits they promise.

The adolescents talked about how popular press schooled them also on how to interpret and project a gendered identity. This was particularly complex for the boys. Men's bodies in advertising frequently project elements of both heterosexual and homosexual styles but the boys were resistant to any association with homosexuality. This shows that teenagers do not succumb passively to dominant media trends – the participants were often discriminating in their internalisation of body images.

All those I spoke to identified the beautiful and defined aesthetic-athletic body as that validated by popular press. But the levels of tone, definition, mass and slenderness that were thought acceptable varied between boys and girls and also varied among them. When asked to select which body in a magazine they liked the best, most could not pick out one specific person. Some chose elements of certain bodies that they would like to have while rejecting others. Their adoption or rejection of a particular size or level of definition shows how the journey from internalising dominant discourses to making them personal practices is individually negotiated and discriminatory.

The teenagers confirmed that they are schooled on the body by popular press insofar as they come to admire the general body type upheld by the press, but this does not mean that they passively emulate it. They were acutely aware of the airbrushing and amelioration that goes into the images portrayed in the media. They were well educated about the time and effort spent on perfecting celebrity bodies and knew this was unrealistic for most people they meet in everyday life. The narratives in this book suggest that the media is only as powerful as adolescents allow it to be. It would be a mistake to imagine them as passive victims of the images they receive. This is dangerous not only in affording media images such power, but also in the amount of agency it takes from adolescents.

Adolescents are reflective and those who featured in this book reflected constantly upon the schooling they received from popular press and negotiated which elements of this schooling they wished to accept for themselves. This depended on how enabling (Giddens, 1991) it promised to be in their localised social contexts. For instance, boys rejected elements of the aesthetic-athletic body if they perceived them to represent homosexuality or femininity. Such representations would not be enabling within their local peer settings. Similarly, some boys accepted broad shoulders because these would be enabling in their rugby playing school, but boys in other schools did not. This suggests that if teenagers' bodies are not shaped by popular press they are shaped by the demands of their peer contexts. However, all their stories highlighted how quests for particular body forms were motivated by a desire to maximise their individual agency.

The role of peers

The most influential schooling teenagers received on body validation was from their peers. While popular press might validate certain bodies and educate teens on the benefits attached to having such a body, it is within localised peer contexts that those benefits are realised. Celebrity bodies might be validated in the press but actual, real adolescent bodies are validated in schools, sports and communities. And they are validated on the basis of how they enable teenagers to achieve accredited status or avoid a discredited one (Goffman, 1963b) within those local settings.

The narratives in this book show how the boys and girls policed each others' bodies when negotiating which teens possessed bodies that were socially enabling. However, the girls exhibited quite different methods from the boys of policing bodies, relentlessly observing bodies and openly analysing what they saw. This provided an open forum about why a status of body validation is assigned to some and not others, or which elements of bodies can be validated while other elements are rejected. This also allowed the girls to monitor their own degree of deviation from the validated bodies and to air their concerns about it.

The boys suggested that it would be detrimental to talk about body concerns or to admire other boys' bodies as this would be perceived as gay or girlie. Their avoidance of talking about body concerns may lead us to presume that teenage boys do not have the same body concerns as girls, but these boys' stories show otherwise. Because boys do not talk about body concerns does not mean they have no regard for body image, particularly a hegemonic, heterosexual image. On the contrary, what this shows is the prevalence of restricted male vocabularies regarding body image in general.

The boys I spoke to did in fact police each other and negotiate the assignment of body validation. However, they did so through macho, physical modes in keeping with popular images of the dominant, hegemonic male. Physical strength was contested through games of wrestling and tussling. This was normal practice among the boys. Body validation was assigned to those who were victorious, perpetuating the notion that boys should express feelings through displays of physical power and suppress airing their feelings in discursive dialogue.

Physical strength, precision, skill and athleticism were all vital to determining the type and level of sports which youths could access. These qualities were also an advantage for girls who wanted to access sports, but social status was not tied specifically to certain sports in the way it was for boys. Sport provided a common geographical and conversational space for boys to gain acceptance but status depended on recognition within only particular team sports. The boys pushed themselves to build the physical qualities that would earn them a team place. The athletic body was validated because it enabled these boys to elevate their social standing among peers, parents, teachers and in their wider communities. They were admired and applauded to such a degree that their athleticism came to be synthesised with aestheticism.

An aesthetic-athletic type body was validated also because it enabled access to romantic relationships. The teens' romantic encounters were underlined by presumed 'hetero-normativity' (Mac an Ghaill, 1994). They discussed the enormous dependency on their bodies for communication in mixed sex encounters. Some suggested that single-sex schooling prevented familiarity and made communication with the opposite sex difficult and uncomfortable so they relied more on their bodies for personal expression.

If acceptance is significantly tied to the body, so too is rejection. While the boys who participated in this study did not speak openly about their peers' admirable physical qualities, they were not restrained about pointing out the flaws or blemishes they perceived. Those thought to be too thin or too fat for body validation were constantly stigmatised at school. Girls participated in such talk too, although often behind the other girls' backs. Labelling indicates another form of policing bodies for validation, accrediting some by discrediting others (Goffman, 1963b). The teens talked about the emotional and physical abuse faced by those who deviate from what is acceptable. This was particularly evident among those who were overweight: their entire personality was targeted and discredited because they were seen as unable to control the body.

As a means of coping with stigmatisation, some self-isolated and others self-segregated into groups of people of similar size. Others self-stigmatised to display to how unharmed they were by their physical labels. Stigmatising underweight and particularly overweight children was normalised within school communities and teasing them, it seemed, was simply an unavoidable aspect of growing up. However, stigmatisation of the body in terms of race, colour and ability was not accepted and this was enshrined in anti-bullying policies in many of the schools. In a practical sense this leaves underweight and overweight teens confused and feeling that disclosing their abuse will not be taken seriously by school authorities. In a theoretical sense it points to a dismembering of the body, where prejudice against certain bodies is accepted and prejudice against other bodies abhorred.

The teenagers received confusing messages from their schools about food also. The body form that enables acceptance and avoids rejection does not exhibit careless indulgence. The curriculum subject SPHE perpetuates the physically fit and regulated body by equating it with health and wellbeing. It educates adolescents on the importance of nutritious food choices. Yet the schools that taught this message failed to provide their students with a serious selection healthy food in their canteens, tuck shops and vending machines.

Eating as a cosmopolitan pursuit enhances people's independence and sociality, so food can be enabling. And the range of food available is exciting and tempting. But careless indulging does not sit easily with the validation of fitness and regulation promoted by the curriculum, the popular press and peers. The teenagers in this study revealed that they thought it necessary to counteract over indulgence. Indulgence was viewed as fulfilling but over indulgence was potentially damaging to body validation. Boys and girls spoke equally about feeling bad if they thought they ate too much, but the boys indicated that they could not discuss these matters with their friends.

After episodes of perceived over-eating the boys and girls exercised more or drank more water or ate a little less in an effort to regain their physical equilibrium. They also talked about the worrying regimes for counter-action used among their peers. Many regarded vomiting much as one would aerobics. It was just a practice used for a time to obtain or regain a certain body size. This highlights how practices such as vomiting infiltrate adolescents' everyday repertoires of regulation. It also raises the question of whether our understanding of purging as a regulatory behaviour should be confined only to considerations of eating disorders.

The role of parents

During the interviews the participants talked about their parents and re-counted in detail their use of gyms and home exercise equipment. Parents played a vital role in schooling their children on the value of working out. Parents and children encouraged and even competed with each other in exercising and training. They schooled one another on techniques to manipulate size or definition. Working out together encouraged friend-ship based relationships between them as they united on a common goal. Many parents took a sizist approach to the body. They were often critical of loose or excess flesh on strangers' bodies, and on their own bodies and their children's. This encourages children to criticise themselves and others along the lines of their parents' criticisms and it highlights how aestheticism and athleticism are common pursuits regardless of age.

Many of the interviewees' parents had toning and exercise equipment at home or were members of a gym. The teens recognised the status attri-buted to working out in gyms from the media, peers and from their parents. Parents who worked out encouraged their children to participate in similar activities, setting a standard and telling them feel-good stories about the gym. They recognised gyms as places where parents and sibl-ings became more enabled through measurable physical improvements. A number of the adolescents I spoke to frequented gyms themselves, not knowing the legal age for admission. They viewed gyms as intensely focused on the body, so that distractions such as conversation were frowned upon.

It seems that parents and their children are united in their quest for an aesthetic-athletic physique. In times dominated by explosive statistics on the growth of obesity yet filled with stories that prejudge fat people, parents who lead their children to exercise by example should perhaps be applauded. What is worrying is that youths who exercise through individualised regimes are required to be consumed by consciousness of their bodies whereas youths who exercise through games of rounders or chasing are often consumed more by the game than by their bodies. The participants focused on burning a specific number of calories rather than on getting a home run. We live in a time where numerical proof of achievements seems to be almost essential for proving our value.

Proving self-value through body validation

I decided to use qualitative techniques to explore whether teenagers feel validated by their bodies and to investigate the social systems that school them on this sense of validation. However, I found that teenagers are schooled to see validation quantitatively. Their views on exercise equipment epitomise this: they wanted to achieve faster times, go further, jump higher, burn more calories, lift heavier weights, become slimmer or in some cases heavier. They spoke of embodied validation through proof of body work. This included body proof of *working on the body* and proof of *working the body* (see Crossley, 2006). Proof of the body's labouring enhanced both physical and psychological self-worth. This book is full of examples of body and embodied validation being quantitatively measured.

The adolescents were schooled by popular press, peers and parents to measure validation through numerical excellence. They learned that body validation came through being given the most compliments, winning the most wrestling matches, scoring the most goals, being invited on most dates, regulating in the most effective ways and so on. Is it any wonder what they feared were quantitative failures? In the general course of conversation, almost all the interviewees referred to their futures being determined by the number of points they receive in their terminal school exam (the Leaving Certificate). They worried incessantly about 'not getting the points'. Obtaining the points was in their eyes a validation of self-worth. They are taught that it is not so much the quality of endeavour that attributes validation but the quantity of achievement. The 'high achiever' is venerated and afforded public recognition, popularity and social standing (Halse, Honey and Boughtwood, 2007:225). In a results driven world individuals are asked to prove that they can take responsibility for their own destiny, so it is hardly surprising that they feel embodied validation depends more on their physical quantities than personal qualities. The weighing scales weighs 'not only bodies, but worthiness' (Shell (2003) cited in Monaghan, 2007:84).

That adolescents are conscious of physical shape and size is not a new discovery. So why is there no comprehensive endeavour by our formal education system to school bodies positively? Schooling on the body takes place within the informal curriculum such as sport and particularly within the hidden curriculum, among peers, in canteens, by grouping policies, through bullying. In the formal curriculum, junior cycle SPHE deals with issues that relate to understanding the body but those teaching this subject often feel inadequately trained to delve too far into serious discussions on body image. Consequently, the lessons tend to focus on combating obesity, asking adolescents to make healthy lifestyle choices and think more about their bodies. But many youths think about little else and are actively schooled into becoming disturbingly bodily conscious.

Adolescents and children sorely need formal schooling on the sociological factors that currently construct, create and clarify – or confuse, contradict and complicate their perceptions of their own bodies. They need schools to challenge size related stigmatisation in the same way they are challenging stigmatisation relating to race, ethnicity, religion and more recently sexual orientation. Long before concerns about race or sexual orientation were spoken of in the Irish context children and teenagers were degraded and ridiculed because of their size. It seems incredible that the issue of size has remained unchallenged and unchartered territory – until this book.

Bibliography

Adam, B. (1996) 'Detraditionalization and the Certainty of Uncertain Futures' in *Detraditionalization*, ed by P. Heelas, S. Lash and P. Morris, Oxford: Blackwell

Adam, B. (2003) 'Reflexive Modernization Temporalized' in *Theory, Culture and Society*, 20 (2): 59-78, London: Sage

Archer, M. (2000) *Being Human: the problem of agency*, UK: Cambridge University Press

Arnot, M. and Mac an Ghaill, M. (2006) *Gender and Education*, London: Routledge

Atkinson, P. et al (2001) *Handbook of Ethnography*, London: Sage

Baker, P (1994) 'Under Pressure: what the media is doing to men' in *Cosmopolitan*, November pp. 129-132

Bartky, S. L. (1990) *Femininity and Domination: studies in the phenomenology of oppression*, London: Routledge

Baudrillard, J. (1982) 'The Beaubourg Effect: implosion and deterrence' in *October*, 20: 3-13

Baudrillard, J. (1983) *Simulations*, New York: Semiotext

Baudrillard, J. (1998) *The Consumer Body: myths and structures*, London: Sage Publications

Bauman, Z. (1989) *Legislators and Interpreters,* Cambridge: Polity Press

Bauman, Z. (1998) *Globalisation: the human consequences*, Cambridge: Polity Press

Bauman, Z. (2005) *Liquid Life,* Cambridge: Polity Press

Beck, U. and Beck-Gernsheim, E. (1996) 'Individualization and 'Precarious Freedoms': perspectives and controversies of a subject-orientated sociology' in *Detraditionalization*, ed. by P. Heelas, S. Lash and P. Morris, Oxford: Blackwell.

Beck, U. (1992) *Risk Society: towards a new modernity*, London: Sage

Beck, U. (2000) 'Risk Society Revisited: theory, politics and research programmes' in *The Risk Society and Beyond: critical issues in social theory*, ed by B. Adam, U. Beck and J. Van Loon. London: Sage

Beck, U., Bonss, W. and Lua, C. (2003) 'The Theory of Reflexive Modernization' in *Theory, Culture and Society,* 20(2): 1-33

Bell, J. (1999) *Doing Your Research Project,* Buckingham: Open University Press

Beynon, J. (2002) *Masculinities and Culture*, Buckingham: Open University Press

Blood, S. K. (2005) *Body Work: the social construction of women's body image*, London: Routledge

Boden, S. (2006) 'Dedicated followers of fashion? The influence of popular culture on children's identities' in *Media, Culture and Society,* 28(1): 289-298

Bordo, S. (1990) 'Reading the Slender Body' in Jacobs, M. (Ed.) *Body Politics: Women and the Discourse of Science,* London: Routledge

Bordo, S. (1993) *Unbearable Weight,* London: University of California Press

Bordo, S. (1994) 'Reading the Male Body' in L. Goldstein *The Male Body: Features, Destinies, Exposures,* University of Michigan

Bourdieu, P. (1990) *In Other Words: essays towards a reflexive sociology*, Cambridge: Polity

Bourdieu, P. (1984) *Distinction: a social critique of the judgement of taste,* translated by R. Nice, London: Routledge and Kegan Paul

Bourdieu, P. and Passeron, L. (1977) *Reproduction in Education, Society and Culture*, Beverly Hills: Sage

Bourdieu, P. and Wacquant, L.J.D. (1992) *An Invitation to Reflexive Sociology*, Cambridge: Polity Press

Bradley, L. (2004) 'Raft of junk food companies keeping Aquatic Centre afloat' in *Sunday Independent,* Sept 5, pp 6

Bray, A. and Colebrook, C. (1998) 'The Haunted Flesh: corporeal feminism and the politics of (dis)embodiment' in *Signs*, 24(11): 35-67

Bruch, H. (1977) *The Golden Cage: the enigma of anorexia nervosa*, London: Harvard University Press

Budgeon, S. (2003) 'Identity as an Embodied Event' in *Body and Society* 9(1): 35-55

Burgess, R. G. (1984) *In the Field: an introduction to field research*, London, Allen and Unwin

Butler, J. (1987) 'Variations on Sex and Gender: Beauvoir, Wittig and Foucault' in S. Benhabib and D. Carroll (eds), *Feminism as Critique: essays on the politics of gender in late capitalist societies,* Cambridge: Polity Press

Byrne, S. (2005) 'Parent Group Slams Christmas Gym Toys' in *The People*, November 20, pp 9

Chambers, I., (1987) 'Maps for the Metropolis: a possible guide to the present' in *Cultural Studies*, 1(1): 1-21

Chernin, K. (1983) *Womansize: tyranny of slenderness*, London: The Women's Press

Childs, F. (2003) 'When bigger is not better' in the *Telegraph Weekend*, October 18, pp 20

Cleary, A. (2005) 'Death Rather than Disclosure: struggling to be a real man' in *Irish Journal of Sociology,* 14(2): 155-176

Connell, R. W. (2002) *Gender,* Cambridge: Polity Press

Connell, R.W. (1995) *Masculinities,* Cambridge UK: Polity Press

Connell, R.W. (2005a) 'Growing up Masculine: rethinking the significance of adolescence in the making of masculinities' in *Irish Journal of Sociology*, 14(2): 11-28

Connell, R.W. (2005b) 'Hegemonic Masculinity: rethinking the concept' in *Gender and Society,* 19(6): 829-259

Connor, M. and Armitage, C. (2000) *The Social Psychology of Food,* Buckingham: Open University Press

Connor, M., Johnson, C. and Grogan, S. (2004) 'Gender, Sexuality, Body Image and Eating Behaviours' in the *Journal of Health Psychology*, 9(4): 505-515

Cook, D. T. (2003) 'Spatial Biographies of Children's Consumption' in the *Journal of Consumer Culture,* 3(2): 147-169

Cook, D. T. and Kaiser, S. B. (2004) 'Betwixt and be Tween: age ambiguity and the sexualization of the female consuming subject' in the *Journal of Consumer Culture*, 4(2): 203-227

Corrigan, P. (1997) *The Sociology of Consumption: an introduction*, London: Sage Publications

Craib, I. (1992) *Anthony Giddens*, London: Routledge

Craik, J. (1994) *The Face of Fashion: cultural studies in fashion*, London: Routledge

Crossley, N. (2001) *The Social Body*, London: Sage

Crossley, N. (2004) 'The Circuit Trainer's Habitus' in *Body and Society*, 10(1): 37-69

Crossley, N. (2005) 'Mapping Reflexive Body Techniques: On Body Modification and Maintenance' in *Body and Society,* 11(1): 1-35

Crossley, N. (2006) 'In the Gym: motives, meaning and moral careers' in *Body and Society*, 12 (3): 23-50

Crotty, M. (1998) *The Foundations of Social Research: meaning and perspectives in the research process,* Thousand Oaks, California: Sage Publications

Dalley-Trim, L. (2007) 'The Boys' Present ... Hegemonic Masculinity: a performance of multiple acts' in *Gender and Education* ed by M. Arnot and M. Mac an Ghaill, London: Routledge

Darcy, J. and Kenny, M. (1997) *Adolescent Development*, Chicago: Brown and Benchmark

Davis, K. (1995) *Reshaping the Female Body: the dilemma of cosmetic surgery*, London: Routledge

De Casanova, E. M. (2004) 'No Ugly Women: concepts of race and beauty among adolescent women in Ecuador' in *Gender and Society,* 18(3): 287-308

Delamont, S. (1992) *Fieldwork in Educational Settings: methods, pitfalls, and perspectives,* London: Falmer.

Demetriou, D. Z. (2001) 'Connell's Concept of Hegemonic Masculinity: a critique' in *Theory and Society*, 30(3): 337-361

Elliot, A. and Lemert, C. (2006) *The New Individualism: the emotional costs of globalisation*, London: Routledge.

Entwistle, J. (2003) 'The Dressed Body' in *Real Bodies: A Sociological Introduction* ed by Mary Evans and Ellie Lee, New York: Palgrave.

Erikson, E. (1963) *Childhood and Society*, New York: Norton.

Evans, M. (2003) 'Real Bodies: An Introduction' in *Real Bodies: a sociological introduction* ed by Mary Evans and Ellie Lee, New York: Palgrave.

Ewen, S. (1990) 'Marketing Dreams: the political elements of style' in *Consumption, Identity and Style: marketing, meaning and the packaging of pleasure*, ed by A. Tomlinson, New York: Routledge

Featherstone, M. (1991a) 'The Body in Consumer Culture' in *The Body: social process and cultural theory* ed. by M. Featherstone, M. Hepworth and B. S. Turner, London: Sage

Featherstone, M. (1991b) *Consumer Culture and Postmodernism*, London: Sage

Featherstone, M. and Burrows, R. (1995) *Cyber space, Cyber bodies, Cyber punk: cultures of technological embodiment,* London: Sage.

Fingerson, L. (2005) 'Agency and the Body in Adolescent Menstrual Talk' in *Childhood,* 12(1): 91-110

Foucault, M. (1977) *Discipline and Punish: the birth of the prison,* Trans A. Sheridan, Harmondsworth: Peregrine

Foucault, M. (1978) *The History of Sexuality: an introduction,* Trans. R. Hurley, Harmondsworth: Penguin

Foucault, M. (1979) *Govermentality,* Brighton: Harvester

Foucault, M. (1980) *Power/Knowledge: selected interviews and other writings, 1927-1977,* Brighton: Harvester

Foucault, M. (1982) 'The Subject and Power' in H. Dreyfus and P. Rainbow, *Michel Foucault: beyond structuralism and hermeneutics,* Chicago University Press

Foucault, M. (1984) 'What is Enlightenment?' in *The Foucault Reader* ed by P. Rainbow, Harmondsworth: Penguin

Foucault, M. (1985) *The Use of Pleasure,* Trans. R. Hurley, Harmondsworth: Penguin

Foucault, M. (1988) 'The Ethic of Care for the Self as a Practice of Freedom' in *The Final Foucault* ed by J. Bernauer and D. Rasmussen Cambridge, Mass.: MIT Press

Frank, A. W. (1990) 'Bringing Bodies Back In: a decade review' in *Theory, Culture and Society,* 7: 131-162

Frank, A.W. (1991) 'For a Sociology of the Body: an analytical review' in *The Body: social process and cultural theory* ed by M. Featherstone, M. Hepworth and B. S. Turner, London: Sage

Frost, L. (2005) 'Theorizing the Young Woman in the Body' in *Body and Society,* 11(1): 63-85

Fussell, S. (1994) 'Bodybuilder Americanus' in *The Male Body* ed by L. Goldstein, University of Michigan Press

Gamman, L. and Makinen, M. (1994) *Female Fetishism: a new look,* London: Lawrence and Wishart

Giddens, A. (1976) *New Rules of Sociological Method: a positive critique of interpretative sociologies,* London: Hutchinson

Giddens, A. (1979) *Central Problems in Social Theory,* London: Macmillan

Giddens, A. (1984) *The Constitution of Society,* Cambridge: Polity Press

Giddens, A. (1989) *Sociology,* Cambridge: Polity Press

Giddens, A. (1991) *Modernity and Self-Identity,* Cambridge: Polity Press

Gill, R., Henwood, K. and McLean C. (2005) 'Body Projects and the Regulation of Normative Masculinity' in *Body and Society,* 11(1): 37-62

Ging, D. (2005) 'A 'Manual on Masculinity'? The consumption and use of mediated images of masculinity among teenage boys in Ireland' in *Irish Journal of Sociology,* 14(2): 29-52

Goffman, I. (1963a) *The Presentation of the Self in Everyday Life,* Hamondsworth: Penguin

Goffman, I. (1963b) *Stigma: notes on the management of a spoiled identity,* London: Penguin

Goffman, I. (1967) *Interaction Ritual: essays on face to face behaviour,* Hamondsworth: Penguin

Gordon, R. A. (1990) *Anorexia and Bulimia: anatomy of a social epidemic*, New York: Blackwell

Gordon, R. A. (2001) 'Eating Disorders East and West: a culture bound system abound' in *Eating Disorders and Culture in Transition* ed. by M. Naser, M. Katzman and R.A. Gordon. Hove: Brunner-Routeledge.

Grogan, S. (1999) *Body Image: understanding body dissatisfaction in Men, Women and Children*, London: Routledge

Halse, C., Honey, A. and Boughtwood, D. (2007) 'The Paradox of Virtue: (re)thinking deviance, anorexia and schooling' in *Gender and Education*, 19(2): 219-235

Haywood, C. and Mac an Ghaill, M. (1997) 'Education and Gender Identity: seeking frameworks of understanding' in *Gender and Education* ed. by M. Arnot and M. Mac an Ghaill. London: Routeledge

Haywood, C., Popoviciu, L., and Mac an Ghaill, M. (2005) 'Feminisation and Schooling: re-masculinisation, gendered reflexivity and boyness' in the *Irish Journal of Sociology,* 14(2): 193-212

Hill, A. (2003) 'Too Much Too Young?' in *The Observer*, Oct, pp 46-55

Hook, G. (2006) 'Schools Rugby: too much too soon or a good grounding for life?' in *The Irish Times*, January 31, pp 13

Ireson, J. and Hallam, S. (2001) *Ability Grouping in Education*, London: Sage

Kehily, M.J. and Nayak, A. (1997) 'Lads and Laughter' in *Gender and Education* ed. by M. Arnot and M. Mac an Ghaill. London: Routeledge

Kern, S. (1975) *Anatomy and Destiny: a cultural history of the human body,* New York: Bobbs-Merrill

Langman, L. (2003) 'Culture, Identity and Hegemony: the body in a global age' in *Current Sociology,* 51(3/4): 223-247

Lasch, C. (1979) *Culture of Narcissism*, New York: W.W. Norton & Company

Lash, S. (1993) in *Bourdieu: critical perspectives*, ed by C. Colhoun, E. Li Puma and M. Postone, Polity Press

Lash, S. (2003) 'Reflexivity as Non-linearity' in *Theory, Culture and Society*, 20(2): 49-57

Leder, D. (1990) *The Absent Body*, Chicago: University of Chicago Press

Leeds Craig, M. and Liberti, R. (2007) ''Cause That's What Girls Do': the making of a feminised gym' in *Gender and Society*, 21(5): 676-699

Lynch, K. and Lodge, A. (1999) 'Essays on School' in *Equality in Education*, ed. by K. Lynch. Dublin: Gill and Macmillan

Lynch, K. and Lodge, A. (2002) *Equality and Power in Schools: redistribution, recognition and representation.* London: Routledge Falmer

Mac an Ghaill, M. (1994) *The Making of Men: masculinities, sexualities and schooling,* Buckingham: Open University press

Mansfield, A. and McGinn, B. (1993) 'Pumping Iron: the muscular and the feminine' in *Body Matters* ed by S. Scott and D. Morgan, London: Falmer Press

Marmot, M. (1994) *Status Syndrome: how social standing affects our heath and longevity*, New York: Henry Holt

Mason, J. (2002) *Qualitative Researching, (2nd ed.)*, London: Sage Publications

McCoy, S., and Smyth, E. (2005) *At Work in School: part-time employment among second-level students*, Dublin: Liffey Press

McNay, L. (1992) *Foucault and Feminism: power, gender and the self*, Cambridge: Polity Press

McNay, L. (1994) *Foucault: a critical introduction*, Cambridge: Polity Press

McRobbie, A. (1991) *Feminism and Youth Culture: from 'Jackie' to 'Just Seventeen'*, London: Macmillan

McSharry, M. (2008) 'Stuck in a Ruck: the impact of rugby on social belonging' in *Belongings: shaping identity in modern Ireland*, ed by M. P. Corcoran and P. Share. Dublin: Institute of Public Administration

Mead, G.H. (1934) *Mind, Self and Society*, Chicago: University of Chicago Press

Merleau-Ponty, M. (1967) *Phenomenology of Perception*, London: Routledge

Messner, M.A. (2002) *Taking the Field: women, men, and sports*, Minneapolis: University of Minnesota Press

Monaghan, L. (1999) 'Creating 'The Perfect Body': a variable project' in *Body and Society*, 2(3): 267-290

Monaghan, L. (2005) 'Big Handsome Men, Bears and Others: virtual constructions of 'fat male embodiment" in *Body and Society*, 11(2): 81-111

Monaghan, L. (2007) 'McDonalizing Men's Bodies? slimming, associated (ir)rationalities and resistances' in *Body and Society,* 13(2): 67-93

Morgan, D. (1993) 'You Too Can Have a Body Like Mine: reflections on the male body and masculinities' in *Body Matters* ed by S. Scott and D. Morgan, London: Falmer Press

Norman, J. *et al.* (2006) *Straight Talk: an investigation of attitudes and experiences of homo-phobic bullying in second-level schools*: Ireland: DCU

Orbach. S. (1988) *Fat is a Feminist Issue,* London: Arrow Books

Probyn, E. (2000) 'Sporting Bodies: dynamics of shame and pride' in *Body and Society*, 6(1): 13-28. London: Sage

Probyn, E. (2004) 'Teaching Bodies: affects in the classroom' in *Body and Society*, 10(4): 21-43

Prout, A. (2000) 'Childhood Bodies: construction, agency and hybridity', *The Body, Childhood and Society* ed by A. Prout Basingstoke: Macmillan

Punch, M. (1994) 'Polities and Ethics in Qualitative Research' in *Handbook of Qualitative Research*, ed by N. K. Denzin and Y. S. Lincoln. Thousand Oakes, CA: Sage

Redmond, S. (2003) 'The White Women in Advertising' in *Journal of Consumer Culture*, 3(2): 170-189

Reimer, B. (1995a) 'The Media in Public and Private Spheres' in *Youth Culture in Late Modernity,* ed by J. Fornas and G. Bolin, London: Sage Publications

Reimer, B. (1995b) 'Youth and Modern Lifestyles' in *Youth Culture in Late Modernity,* ed by J. Fornas and G. Bolin, London: Sage Publications

Rice, F.P. (1999) *The Adolescent*, Boston: Allyn and Bacon

Ritzer, G. (1992) *Sociological Theory,* New York: McGraw Hill

Ritzer, G. (1993) *McDonaldization of Society*, Thousand Oaks, CA: Pine Forge

Sacker, I. and Zimmer, M. (1987) *Dying to Be Thin,* New York: Warner

Sassatelli, R. (2000) 'Interaction Order and Beyond: a field analysis of body culture within fitness gyms' in *Body Modification* ed by M. Featherstone, London: Sage

Sayers, J. (2003) 'Feeding the Body' in *Real Bodies: a sociological introduction* ed by Mary Evans and Ellie Lee, New York: Palgrave

Schlosser, E. (2002) *Fast Food Nation,* London: Penguin

Schutt, R. K. (2004) *Investigating the Social World: the process and practice of research*, London: Pine Forge Press

Sennett, R. (1994) *The Flesh and the Stone: the body and the city in western civilisation,* New York: W.W. Norton

Shilling, C. (1993) *The Body and Social Theory,* London: Sage

Shilling, C. (2003) *The Body and Social Theory (Second Edition)*, London: Sage

Shilling, C. (2005) *The Body in Culture, Technology and Society,* London: Sage

Silverman, D. (2000) *Doing Qualitative Research: a practical handbook*, London, Sage Publications

Steinberg, L. (1996) *Adolescence*, New York: McGraw-Hill

Swain, J. (2003) 'How Young Boys Become Somebody: the role of the body in the construction of masculinity' in *British Journal of Sociology of Education*, 24(3): 299-314

The Report of the National Taskforce on Obesity (2005) *Ireland: Department of Health and Children*

Thomas, C. (2003) 'The Disabled Body' in *Real Bodies: a sociological introduction* ed by Mary Evans and Ellie Lee, New York: Palgrave.

Thompson, J.B. (1989) 'The Theory of Structuration' in *Social Theory in Modern Societies: Anthony Giddens and his critics*, ed by D. Held and J.B. Thompson, Cambridge: Cambridge University Press

Tomlinson, A. (1990) 'Consumer culture and the aura of the commodity' in *Consumption, Identity and Style: marketing, meaning and the packaging of pleasure,* ed by A. Tomlinson, New York: Routledge

Turner, B. (1984) *The Body and Society: explorations in social theory,* Oxford: Basil Blackwell

Turner, B. (1992) *Regulating Bodies,* London: Routledge

Turner, B. (1996) *The Body and Society: explorations in social theory, (second ed.)* Oxford: Basil Blackwell

Turner, B. (1999) 'The Possibility of Primitiveness: towards a sociology of body marks in cool societies' in *Body and Society,* 5(2-3): 39-50

Turner, T. (1994) 'Bodies and Anti-bodies: flesh and fetish in contemporary social theory' in *Embodiment and Experience: the existential ground of culture and self,* ed by T.J. Csordas, New York: Cambridge University Press

Varga, I. (2005) 'The Body – The New Sacred? the body in hypermodernity' in *Current Sociology*, 53(2): 209-235

Wacquant, L.J.D. (1994) 'Why Men Desire Muscles' in *Body and Society,* 1(1): 163-180

Weber, M. (1965) *The Protestant Ethic and the Spirit of Capitalism,* New York: Charles Scribner and Sons.

Weedon, C. (1987) *Feminist Practice and Poststructuralist Theory,* Oxford: Basil Blackwell

Williams, J. (2005) *50 Facts that Should Change the World,* UK: Icon Books

Wolff, J. (1990) *Feminine Sentences: essays on women and culture,* Basingstoke: Macmillan

Young, I.M. (1990) *Justice and the Politics of Difference,* Princeton, NJ: Princeton University Press

Index

objectified capital 43, 47
overweight *see* fat, obesity

parents 6, 43, 89, 99, 102,
109-113, 124, 132-133
peer groups 43-44, 46-51, 57-
61, 64, 82-83, 129, 131
physical impression, 57-65
policing bodies 29-32, 38-41,
116, 129-130
popular press 9-15, 17-28,
29-31, 127-129
predictability 92, 95-105, 107,
112, 117-118, 123, 132
prestige 49-56, 61, 63-64,
130

reflexive body techniques
117-118
regulation 30, 87, 91-96, 98-
105, 107, 108-124, 131-
133
rejection *see* stigmatisation
research methods 4-5
romantic relationships 57-65,
130

segregatio, 82-85, 131
self-consciousness 3, 9, 29-
31, 58-60, 69, 73, 79-80,
82-83, 133-134
self-enclosure 81-82, 84-85,
131
self-stigmatisation 83-85, 131
self-worth *see* embodied
validation
semiformal subsystems *see*
peer groups
siblings 107, 109-113
single-sex schools 2, 4, 58-
59, 130
sizism 75-76, 97, 132
social constructionism 108-
109
social class 10, 21-22, 92-93,
102, 109
SPHE *see* curriculum
sport 16-17, 44-56, 64, 72,
89, 103, 113, 130
status *see* prestige
stigmatisation 67-85, 131
structuration theory 13-14,
108

thinness 15-19, 32-33, 70-74
see also aesthetic-athletic
body
tweenagers 9

underweight *see* thinness

weight training 107-109, 111
working out *see* exercise